FACING THE ACTIVE SHOOTER:

Guidelines for the Armed Citizen Defender

2018 Updated Edition

CR Williams

Copyright 2013 In Shadow In Light
Copyright Revised Edition 2014 In Shadow In Light
Copyright 2nd Revision 2015 In Shadow In Light
Copyright 2016 Update In Shadow In Light
Copyright 2017 Update In Shadow In Light
Copyright 2018 Updated Edition In Shadow In Light

Introduction: History Repeating

Mumbai, Nairobi, Aurora, Charleston, Paris, Orlando are some of the more recent ones. There have been others besides these. They won't be the only ones, either. Someday, somewhere, some-when, one or more people will enter a place full of other people and start shooting them down or blowing them up or both. Why they do that will sometimes be open to question. That they will do that, someday, somewhere, some-when, is not.

Active shooters have come before.

They will come again.

The US Department of Homeland Security defines an Active Shooter as *"an individual actively engaged in killing or attempting to kill people in a confined and populated area; in most cases, active shooters use firearm[s] and there is no pattern or method to their selection of victims."*

(I respectfully disagree with the last part of this definition. Recent attacks have indeed displayed a pattern in victim selection by the shooters. The primary patterns I observe relate to selection of victims by cultural [including sub-cultural groupings within the larger umbrella of national or regional culture], religious, and workplace affiliation.)

It is a crime of violence, but not the same as criminal violence. It is sometimes focused, but not always, and even when it has a focus it often broadens past the initial victim selection. It takes advantage of our wish and tendency to congregate and of the tendency of most people to not want to think that anything bad could ever happen to them and/or where they are.

If you are reading this, you are not "most people". If you are reading this, you have at least begun to acknowledge the possibility that bad things do happen to good people and that bad things happen and can happen anywhere and everywhere. If you are reading this, you are at least curious about if not actively seeking some guidelines or a framework about how to deal with this kind of irrational attack against you and your loved ones.

This booklet is an effort to provide such a framework. It is designed to provide you with a group of concepts that you can use in your planning, training, and preparation for countering this kind of attack. It is oriented toward someone who has some knowledge of shooting and perhaps some basic training in the tactics and strategies of the armed encounter but no specialized background or even basic military or law enforcement training or experience. It is written, in other words, for most of us who have decided to carry a gun when and where we can, who have decided to take responsibility for our own defense against attack, and who want to know as much as we can about how to defend themselves and our loved ones if we are attacked.

The outline and supporting briefs that follow this introduction are based on open source information from studies of active shooting events that took place primarily within the Continental United States, and from sources as varied as videos posted to Internet sites, news service and Internet blog reports and gleanings from other sources. Nothing used in this report is classified. This was combined with, filtered through, and considered against everything I have heard, seen, read, or experienced under the guidance of some of the most capable and dangerous men I know or know of. I have organized it, ordered it, added ideas and concepts and thoughts of my own, and given it a direction to create a set of suggestions about how best to respond if you ever find yourself caught up in such a life-threatening event.

Understand when reading this that only concepts, broad strategies, outlines and ideas are or indeed can be offered in this format. There is no hard-and-fast rule-set, no do-this-here/do-that-there kind of specific suggestion or instruction offered. Everyone's situation is and will be unique. Everyone starts from a different point even if they are in the same room of the same building when an attack starts. Specifics are not offered here because they cannot be offered here.

Understand also that this is a work in progress. As new or additional information comes in, as new concepts and strategies useful to the average concealed-weapons carrier are developed, this work will be modified to add that. Anything demonstrated as useless or unworkable will be removed. This process will be ongoing.

Two points have to be made before moving on to the subject of this text. **One: There are no guarantees**. I have tried to organize workable concepts and workable strategies that will give you something to build on as you plan and prepare for this type of attack. There is always an element of uncertainty about a fight, though, even when everything is done properly. Reality is, most of the time if you fight better and work your plan, tactics, and techniques better than your opponent, you are more likely to win and survive. Reality also is, you can do everything perfectly and still die. That doesn't mean you don't study, train, and practice. All of that increases your chances of winning a fight. To say that any given thing will guarantee your victory, however, is to tell you a lie, and I refuse to do that to you. To tell yourself that any given thing will guarantee victory is to perhaps fatally deceive yourself, and I hope you will refuse to do that to yourself.

Two: As there can be no guarantees, there can be no liability assumed by anyone involved in the production or distribution of this work. Your safety and the results of your practice of anything you see here is your own responsibility. The author and all others involved in any way with the development, production, and distribution of this material disclaim, refuse, and deny any and all assumption of liability as a result of

the understanding, misunderstanding, interpretation, misinterpretation, use or misuse of the material contained herein.

Finally: All material here is either my production, public-access information, or I have permissions from the originator or producer of the material to use it here. All that said: Here it is. I hope it helps you. Good luck.

CR Williams

CONTENTS

Introduction

The Nature of the Threat

Multiple Shooters and the Pistol-vs-Rifle Question

Bombs

Preparing For Action

Modifying the Carry Gun

Targeting the Head

Vehicles

Blades

When You Don't Have A Gun

Truck Guns

Examples
Covert Ready
Moving With the Gun
Close-In Positions
Supported Shooting

Facing an Active Shooter: The Outline

After It's Over

Resources

What I Think Is Coming

Last Word

The Nature of the Threat

In the US the most likely active-shooter threat you might face is still a single male carrying more than one gun.

Overseas, reports indicate a higher likelihood of multiple shooters in a single incident. Since the only reports most of us see from overseas are the ones deemed significant enough to make the news, it seems unlikely that the majority of incidents in other countries involve more than one shooter. The probability of multiple shooters still remains higher outside than inside CONUS (COntiNental US) as of the time of this writing. HOWEVER: I believe that assaults on the model of the Mumbai, Nairobi, and Paris attacks will be made in the US in the future. Keep this in mind as you make your mental and physical preparation to meet this threat.

You will most likely face the shooter(s) inside a building. Open-air shootings remain rare so far. Buildings offer advantages and disadvantages to both sides during an attack. The attacker gets a cluster of targets that can be channeled and cornered and, if he chooses to use it, cover and concealment to take advantage of. You get cover and concealment, multiple covered routes for exit or counterattack, and additional resources to use in setting up your defense and/or counterattack. Both of you get the "fog of war" effect that comes from not being able to see everything and everyone you want or need to see.

Some shooters go in with a plan, some do not. There are indications that some shooters study previous incidents and learn from them. When plans are made that planning can be extensive and conducted for long periods of time before the shooting starts. Individual shooters very often have some relationship (family, community, workplace or a combination of those three) to the group and/or area they attack. In the case of terror attacks there is often a study of the target(s) in advance and planning and preparation for the attack can be quite extensive.

Reports of shooters preparing the area of the attack in advance are still rare. Actions such as blocking exits or setting traps in and around the area in advance of the attack are still in the reported minority. (Within the Continental United States.)

Shooters are driven by either mental illness, emotional disturbance, ideology, or (most likely) a combination of at least two of those factors. This will normally not be important to you, but if the situation plays out for longer than the average incident time, it is possible that you can use this to gain an advantage. This does not mean that you can reason or negotiate with them. In no case should you expect empathy or mercy from anyone engaged in an active-shooting attack. It is important to remember that an active shooter is not rational (even though the execution of their attack may be). Any attempt to reason with them is almost certainly doomed to failure. In the case of terrorist attacks you should also expect the attackers to be using drugs to increase their endurance and resistance to pain and to reduce fear or anxiety.

The majority of active shooters continue shooting and killing until they are opposed. It is important to remember this. Less than one in five in an NYPD study of active shooter incidents in the US were stopped by anything other than external force being brought to bear. An interesting point is that once even mild opposition or the threat of opposition was encountered, most active shooters kill themselves. Very few attempt to engage responding individuals or units. Very few are captured alive.

Something else reported fairly often (not a majority of the time, but enough to make note of it) is that at some point in the event the shooter will have a problem with the gun. There will be a malfunction or a need to reload and the shooter will fumble with the weapon getting or trying to get it back into play.

There are other aspects to the threat you might face that don't involve the shooter:

- Other people.
- Responders.

Once the shooting starts, people will react. Most are likely to attempt to avoid the shooter in some way. This could be by locking themselves in somewhere or barricading the shooter's access in some way. It could be by concealing themselves in some way. It could be by trying to escape, to run away from the shooter. This could inhibit or prevent some or all of your own efforts to escape or engage.

Law enforcement response must also be considered. The longer the event takes, the more likely that officers will enter the scene attempting to find and neutralize the shooter. They will come in hard and fast and they will be ready to shoot anyone they perceive as a threat. If you are not aware of this possibility, you could be in danger from other good guys.

There is also a possibility that other non-military/non-LE personnel will be present who will respond to the attack. (Off-duty police or military who are armed also fall into this category.) This presents both a threat in that they might perceive you as the shooter by mistake, and an opportunity in that they could be combined with to more easily overcome the shooter. The fastest way to differentiate between shooter and other responder at this time appears to be how they act. Put simply, a responder will not act like an active shooter or vice versa.

To summarize the "average" threat:

You will likely be facing a single person with at least two guns inside a building that they have at least some familiarity with. They will move through the building engaging targets of opportunity either after shooting someone specific or right from the start. Once they start shooting, they won't stop until something or someone stops them.

To summarize the minimal threat you should prepare to deal with:

A single shooter with more than one gun that has planned their attack and prepared the area such that easy exits and entry by responders are blocked. They will use rudimentary tactical movement techniques while engaging targets of opportunity. They will have basic familiarization with shooting and weapon operation. They may engage opposition for a time but most will soon pull back a little or stop where they are and commit suicide once they meet any opposition. (It is important, however, that you not assume that a couple of shots in their direction or the mere display of a weapon is going to provoke them to suicide. You must set up for a full-on fight and must assume that if you don't stop them cold with your first shot(s), that they will fight you until they can't any more. Assume anything less and you may die.)

The worst-case scenario at this time appears to be:

A group of shooters heavily armed that has surveyed the area of their attack and planned the process of the attack. They will prepare the area shortly before or during the initial phase of the assault to block and/or kill responders and targets inside the area of the assault. The group will split into smaller units to assault multiple targets and/or from multiple directions. They will take prisoners and prepare to fight responding units and prolong the event, but will likely not plan to either escape or have any of their prisoners survive the assault. (Think about that last part before you decide to surrender to them.)

The important common factor in all cases: The attacker(s) do not often expect to survive and aim to kill as many people as they can before they die.

Some additional information based on academic studies:

Duration of average active shooter incident is 12 minutes.

37% last less than five minutes. (Note that average police response time in the United States is reported to be five minutes.)

49% of attackers committed suicide either at the conclusion of the event or when challenged.

34% were arrested.

17% were killed by responders.

51% of the attacks studied occurred in the workplace.

17% occurred in a school.

17% occurred in a public place.

6% occurred in a religious establishment.

2% of the shooters bring improvised explosive devices (IEDs) as an additional weapon.

10% of cases the shooter stops and walks away.

20% of cases the shooter goes mobile, moving to another location.

43% of the time, the crime is over before police arrive.

57% of shootings, an officer arrives while shooting is still underway.

49 percent of the time attacks ended before police arrived.

56 percent of attacks were ongoing when police arrived.

Officers had to use force to stop the killing.

This is the broad outline of the threat environment that an active shooter or shooters creates according to published reports and studies I have seen.

Published reports and studies aside, it is my opinion that it won't be long before we see one or more large-scale, more sophisticated attacks in the US like we have seen in Paris, Brussels, and now Istanbul. The enemy we face is not stupid and they are learning. I suspect they will apply that learning here sooner rather than later. In that case, expect an attack from multiple groups either at a single location or in different locations sing both guns and bombs and coordinated by men and women with experience and prior training for the operation.

I don't believe that to be a matter of if as much as when it happens within CONUS.

Multiple Shooters and the Pistol-vs-Rifle Question

An analysis of recent incidents and what it might mean if you're caught in one like them.

Although this is addressed in a general way in the outline portion of this book I am adding this to address certain comments I have read on some Internet forums. Those comments are appearing in response to every reported incident so far that includes a large group or more than one shooter armed with a rifle. The comments when they appear take the form of expressed doubt that a (usually) single person armed with a pistol has a reasonable chance against more than one (sometimes just one) attacker armed with a rifle. Sometimes those expressed doubts are small and sometimes they are large. Since I believe it is only a matter of time before such a group attack is carried out somewhere within the United States as it already has been elsewhere I wish to take a moment to address this specifically.

First consider this list of some of the common characteristics of multiple-shooter attacks that can be discerned based on published reports to date:

- However large the <u>total</u> number of attackers has been in any incident, the largest number of attackers reported at any <u>one</u> place has been three, possibly four. The average

number of shooters actually present at any one location is <u>two</u>.
- Even where the group attacked a single location the group is reported to have split up, usually in the early stages of the attack, into teams of two. They might recombine after they have swept the area they entered or at a single location in the case of an attack on separate targets later, but the early stage of all reported attacks so far indicate an early separation into small teams.
- This is one of the first key points you need to know to better understand what you may face and how you can best face it.
- Unless they all enter the same point of a building and immediately open fire and unless you are at that point of entry you will probably (not certainly, but probably) not face more than two shooters at any one time.

- Actual shooting occurs primarily at what we consider to be 'pistol range'—within (often well within) twenty yards or across the length or width of a large room. Even when the attacker(s) could have shot from much greater distance, the majority according to reports came in close before opening fire.
  - Most of your fight-oriented training is oriented toward the usual range of engagement of the rifle-armed attacker.
- The longest distance an attacker has fired at in reported incidents is impossible for me to determine based on available reports. It does not at this time appear to be more than fifty yards, perhaps seventy-five yards at the time of this writing.
  - Still well within the ability of 9mm-and-larger pistols to hit, disable, and kill over that distance.

- - It is easy for most competent shooters to learn to hit at longer distances and beyond if they are not already capable of doing so.
- In reported incidents so far volume of fire appears to account for more casualties than accuracy of fire.
  - Even if they've already started shooting in your direction you may well have time to access your weapon and return fire if you don't panic. (Assuming there is no cover within immediate reach.)
- There is likely to be a pause or reduction in the shooting at some point if the shooting goes on more than a few seconds.
  - Magazine changes that interrupt their shooting or outright malfunctions of the rifle are commonly reported.
  - There is opportunity each time this occurs for movement and/or for counterattack.
- So far the most common type of rifle reported where shooters use rifles overseas is the ubiquitous AK-47. Inside the US it is more likely to be an AR or AR-variant design.
  - Military versions are select-fire, civilian-available versions semi-auto only.
  - It is possible to modify a semi-auto rifle to select-fire or fully automatic modes.
  - AK-47: Heavy round that has good ability to penetrate the walls and doors you will find in most buildings. AR: Less able to penetrate than an AK but don't underestimate that.
    - Most types of 9mm and larger pistol rounds will also penetrate those same walls and doors.
  - Rifles should be respected like any weapon but do not assign them power and capability they do not have.

- Military-type load bearing gear is sometimes reported being used.
    - Chest rigs or load-bearing vests most often carrying spare magazines and some supporting equipment.
    - More common are simple backpacks or other bags.
    - Loaded magazines in chest rigs or vests are not equivalent to body armor but may slow down or stop handgun rounds. That should not prevent you from shooting where the load-bearing equipment is if that is the only or best target you have. If you can, however, go above that to the upper chest, throat, and head.
    - Usually reported is a backpack carrying additional ammunition for their weapon(s) as well as food and water and other items meant to support and sustain their attack for as long as possible.
    - Backpacks can also contain explosives and be rigged as bombs. This will be addressed later.
    - Backpacks are likely more often used because they are very commonly carried in the general population and so are less suspicious and easier to maneuver to and between targets with without arousing as much suspicion.
    - Also because carrying capacity greater than chest rigs or load-carrying vests.

It is important to understand that, especially if you have some training in counter-offensive shooting techniques and tactics and you are a competent shot, you have what you need to successfully engage and defeat a rifle-armed attacker. Large-scale changes or totally different approaches to your training are not required. The main change is in the way you think about dealing with this kind of attack instead of a 'normal' criminal assault.

Here are some things to consider when planning and practicing your response to this kind of assault:

- If caught in the open and if you can, move sideways to or at an angle toward the flank of the shooter(s) quickly to get out of the arc of fire. (This also allows you to attack from the flank and put at least one shooter behind another temporarily to reduce your immediate threat.) At least angle away as sharply as you can. Only move directly away from any shooter if there is no other option or if the best cover is close behind you.
- You can't depend on them being bad shots every time. If you can't escape or get to hard cover immediately you need to be able to get on target and get hits as quickly as you can no matter what.
- Wherever and whenever possible set an ambush. The most powerful weapon is useless to someone that is disabled or killed before they have a chance to use it.

Since the time of the last update we have seen at least two incidents where the shooter was confirmed to be wearing body armor. We therefore have to consider the possibility that the one we face will also be wearing it or something else resistant to shots from commonly-carried handguns.

- You must be prepared to place shots in the head of any shooter on the instant.
- Negate the armor by avoiding it in your target point selection.
- If possible, make the head shot the first shot of the engagement by default.
- Soft armor will still transmit impact force from a round (blunt-force trauma) and may shake them up mentally. This presents the possibility of momentarily fixing them in place with a fast shot or two so that you can transition to a higher target with increased chance of making the stopping shot.

- Going low before you go high is an option whether there is a known armor or bomb vest or if the first shot(s) to the upper body don't stop the attack. Goal here is to slow them down or bring them down completely to make it easier to fully neutralize them with a shot or shots to the head.

Bombs

Shooters according to latest incident reports are employing bombs of various types and in various combinations in addition to firearms. Some consideration of combination attacks with guns and explosives is therefore advisable.

Bombs can be placed ahead of time at the target of the attack, placed during the attack itself, or left behind as and if the attackers leave the scene of an attack. Attackers may also be wearing bombs in the form of belts or vests. Bombs may (probably will be) concealed in some way—inside a package or backpack or other item that a person might carry in the area of the attack or placed in something in that area beforehand (shrubbery or garbage cans, for example). Belts or vest will be worn beneath clothing to conceal them. (Belts don't carry as much explosive as a vest but are easier to conceal.)

Let's be realistic about this. If the attackers have given much thought to concealment of pre-placed bombs at all you will be unlikely to see them, especially as you are moving to escape, avoid or engage them during an attack. What you can do is scan for things that are out of place as you move through the area and check exit points for both locks and/or chains the attacker(s) have added and/or explosive packages attached or connected to doors. Understand and accept that these scans cannot be thorough if you're moving as fast as you likely will be and that you cannot take time to make thorough searches if you are escaping a group of shooters (assuming you know how to properly search an area for explosives). Risks have to be accepted no matter what. When engaging anyone that you suspect or know to be carrying or wearing a bomb prioritize two things if possible: Distance and head shots. There are several reasons for this:

- The explosive may be sensitive to kinetic impact and you want to avoid setting it off. Some 'home-made' explosive compounds are known to be sensitive in this way.
- Dead-man switches are rare. For practical reasons suicide bombers tend to use some sort of positive activation such as a rocker switch or touching wires together. If a shot or shots to the body does not kill them immediately they may still be able to detonate their device.
- There may be a backup with a remote detonator who will set the bomb off if the carrier goes down. This is also why you do not want to approach a downed attacker even if it appears clear otherwise to do so. (And even if they are not apparently carrying explosives. There may be something you can't see. Don't take a chance on it.)

The best option, if it is available, is shooting from distance from behind good cover. Remember to move after a successful engagement. The attacker(s) you stop should not be assumed to be isolated. Reposition or escape the area even if you have no evidence of other hostile presence.

Even given that concealed pre-placed bombs are unlikely to be easily seen you should still be on the lookout for anything out of place in any area you're moving through. Stray packages, boxes, backpacks or bags could be dropped by people fleeing the shooters or by the shooters or someone working with them. Don't approach anything setting out any closer than you have to and certainly don't touch it or try to pick it up. Odds are it won't kill you, but the odds that it will are not zero, and we are and will be seeing a bigger chance that more than guns will be used in the future. Be wary and avoid giving in to curiosity about things.

When dealing with a possible bomb, placed or carried, distance is definitely your friend in the absence of good solid cover. The danger here is not as much shrapnel, which many think about when they think about bombs, but the blast wave. The blast wave will kill as or more readily than shrapnel will and covers a much larger area than shrapnel does because it spreads out without a gap or break from the explosion. It will cause an overpressure effect that will disrupt your internal organs. Heat from the explosion within the blast zone will cause severe injury and death and start secondary fires that might threaten you if you have to move through the area of an explosion afterwards. The area where a bomb blast will be lethal or damaging depends on the amount of explosive in the bomb. This chart from the Department of Homeland Security provides some guidelines for how far away you need to be to avoid damaging effects:

BOMB THREAT STAND-OFF CHART

Threat Description Improvised Explosive Device (IED)	Explosives Capacity[1] (TNT Equivalent)	Building Evacuation Distance[2]	Outdoor Evacuation Distance[3]
Pipe Bomb	5 LBS	70 FT	1200 FT
Suicide Bomber	20 LBS	110 FT	1700 FT
Briefcase/Suitcase	50 LBS	150 FT	1850 FT
Car	500 LBS	320 FT	1500 FT
SUV/Van	1,000 LBS	400 FT	2400 FT
Small Moving Van/ Delivery Truck	4,000 LBS	640 FT	3800 FT
Moving Van/ Water Truck	10,000 LBS	860 FT	5100 FT
Semi-Trailer	60,000 LBS	1570 FT	9300 FT

1. These capacities are based on the maximum weight of explosive material that could reasonably fit in a container of similar size.
2. Personnel in buildings are provided a high degree of protection from death or serious injury; however, glass breakage and building debris may still cause some injuries. Unstrengthened buildings can be expected to sustain damage that approximates five percent of their replacement cost.
3. If personnel cannot enter a building to seek shelter they must evacuate to the minimum distance recommended by Outdoor Evacuation Distance. These distance is governed by the greater hazard of fragmentation distance, glass breakage or threshold for ear drum rupture.

Note that the evacuation distance in buildings assumes that you will be putting walls and internal barriers between you and the bomb. Going from one end of a mall to the other but staying in the open center court is not going to equal seventy feet of distance inside an office complex, for example.

Note the long outdoor distancing required for safety. For a pipe bomb the distance is 400 <u>yards</u> and it goes up quickly from there. The only substitute for distance is solid cover.

If you get warning or suspect that an explosion is about to happen and you can't get far enough away and can't get to cover then get as low on the ground as you can with your feet together and pointed toward the bomb location and make sure you keep your mouth open. This will put the most non-vital parts of the body between you and the bomb and help to keep your eardrums from rupturing. Don't stand up and think you can go down or duck when you see the explosion. You're not fast enough. And if there is even a small depression you can get to before anything goes off, get into it. Even partial cover is better than no cover.

Greg Ellifritz of Active Response Training offers some additional information that could help you identify and avoid bombs and bombers:

"Sometimes you might be able to identify a suicide bomber before he detonates. Here's what to look for:

- Clothing that is bulky or excessive for the weather (to hide the bomb).
- Hands hidden (possibly holding the switch to detonate the bomb).
- A strange chemical odor or excessive cologne to cover up that smell.
- The bomber is focused, but unresponsive. Suicide bombers often have the "1000 yard stare" and are usually unresponsive to questions or commands.
- Heavy luggage or backpacks that don't fit the situation.
    - The average weight of a bomb used by a suicide bomber is around 20 lbs. The Madrid train bombers all had very heavy backpacks. The Moscow bomber placed his bomb in a rolling suitcase. Not all the bombers wear their bombs.
- Nervousness, excessive sweating, or repeated mumbling of a prayer or mantra.
- Exposed wires anywhere on a person's body.

- Repeated attempts to avoid security checkpoints and/or police officers.

...What should you do if you notice a person with one or more of these descriptors or even a suspicious package? GET AWAY! Time, distance, and shielding are the only defense. Realize that a 20lb suicide bomb vest loaded with shrapnel is dangerous within 400 meters. That's a long distance! Recent research has determined that 15 meters (about 50 feet) is the distance that means the difference between life and death in most suicide bombing incidents. If you are within 15 meters of the bomber when he detonates, you will likely die. If you are beyond 15 meters, you will likely live, but may be seriously injured. Ultimately, whether you live or die depends on the terrain, the type of bomb and shrapnel and how far away from the bomb you are. The farther away you can get, the better off you will be. Ideally, distance combined with some type of cover that will stop shrapnel and projectiles is best. For the 500kg Oslo car bomb, people were likely hit by shrapnel up to 1/2 mile away!

...After the Engagement or Detonation

Whether you decide to shoot or even if the terrorist blows the bomb before you engage, there are a few things that you should be thinking about...

Often terrorist bomber have "handlers", "dispatchers", or security people assigned to them. The role of these people is to protect the bomber in case anyone intervenes or to detonate the bomb if the terrorist gets cold feet. Watch out for these people! Scan for anyone who appears to be paying undue attention to the situation, especially if that person is behind some type of cover or at a discreet distance away. If you choose to shoot, you may be in a fight with more than just the bomber!

...Look for people watching who are not scared or stunned. The Russian handlers were all on cell phones. That may be another tip off. Most modern terrorist bombs use cell phones as triggers (switches). The handlers may be on the phone reporting to their superiors or they may be planning to set off another bomb.

...If you shoot the bomber, or even if you just see the bomber blow up, do not approach the body! You don't know if there is another bomb planted on him, if the primary bomb is on a time delay, or if it is command detonated by another person. Keep far away! Try to get everyone else away too. Move quickly to cover after you shoot or he blows up.

Reportedly, the Russian bomb was triggered by the act of the bomber opening the suitcase. Resist the temptation to open any potential bomb to see what it is. If you think it's a bomb, then treat it like a bomb! Get away and get to cover!

...Beware of secondary devices. Oftentimes bombers will use more than one bomb. The original bomb is just designed to create havoc and bring in first responders. A second bomb placed in an evacuation zone, obvious command post staging area, or near the body is designed to injure more people, specifically fire and police officers.

After one bomb goes off, look for items that seem out of place...discarded baggage or backpacks, strange pieces of trash, or recently disturbed ground. If you see any of these things, get away from them! If a bomb goes off, don't evacuate into a parking lot. Cars are the easiest place to hide large amounts of explosive for a secondary device. One very common tactic is to place a small bomb in or near a building or public area. The terrorist knows that the small bomb will trigger an evacuation. He will then place a bigger bomb at the evacuation site to blow up all of the evacuees. I'm repeating myself, but this is very important...NEVER EVACUATE TO A PARKING LOT! It's too easy to hide a (big) bomb in a car. Get far away from anything that may conceal a secondary device!"

So in a nutshell:

The use of bombs as a primary or secondary means of death and destruction in conjunction with firearms must now be considered. Bombs may pave the way for guns or guns may open the way for bombs.

Bombs may be emplaced ahead of time or carried to the target by the bomber.

There may be more than one bomb, placed so as to catch people evacuating from the area of a previous explosion and/or those responding to the first bomb blast or report of a bomb.

Distance and cover are needed whether you are escaping a known or suspected bomb or bomber or if you have decided or been forced to engage them.

If you engage a known or suspected bomber, prioritize destruction of the brain.

If you successfully bring a known or suspected bomber down, make sure they are really incapable of action and get away. Get distance and/or cover between you and them as quickly as possible.

If you suspect bombs and bombers are present, expect that they will have support and handlers in the area in sight of them.

Preparing For Action

There are some things you can do to prepare against the possibility that you will face an active shooter. Many, perhaps most, of the things that you can do to prepare for this specific situation will also help you prepare for more "normal" defensive situations against criminal assault or actions taken against you by disturbed individuals and are preparations that should be undertaken by anyone who carries a weapon for defense.

Assume the attitude.

The basis of the attitude for dealing with an active shooter, especially if escape is not an option, is summed up in this phrase: "I must FIGHT. No holding back!" As stated in the threat synopsis and the core outline, an active shooting is not a rational crime and an active shooter is not a rational person. Very few active shooters have ever escaped or been captured alive. Historically, most have committed suicide if they were not killed by the first encounter with armed resistance. Very few apparently plan to be alive when it is over. The only choice you have, therefore, if you can't or don't escape is whether you will attempt to end their killing sooner rather than later. Historically speaking, the only way you will do that is to either kill them or provoke them into killing themselves. Once committed to fighting them, you must go (intelligently) all-out until they are unable, one way or the other, to continue their killing spree.

That given, the next part of the attitude involves you making sure that you are able and, more importantly, willing to commit yourself to such an intelligently-guided all-out counter-attack. Ability is the easiest part of this. Because of the nature of this kind of event, some concealed-weapon carriers are hesitant to understand that much of what they already know how to do is as applicable to an active shooting as it is to an armed assault in the store parking lot. There is not some special set of tactics or specific techniques that must be learned just so you can deal with this specific situation. You have a lot of what you need already. There are some things, however, that you can add to the basic skill-set that will be more helpful for this. This will be covered later. But these skills and skill-sets, while helpful, are not absolutely needed. What you most need, you already have. Understand that now.

Ability, though, is useless without the will to drive it. When thinking about the active shooter and how you respond to them, there is a question that I think you need to answer:

If you are not engaged directly, will you seek them out with intent to engage them?

Take a little time to consider this. Immediate defense is one thing. Moving to the sound of the guns and toward someone that is actually shooting people and who might, if you don't get them first, be shooting at you is not something everyone can do. It is also true that all of the pre-event determination you have may not suffice to get your feet moving in the reality of the actual event. I believe it will be harder, however, if you have not decided beforehand whether you will advance or not. So consider it now and at least lay the foundation for an on-scene decision later. Consider this, either way: By having a weapon on you, you have a chance of ending the killing far sooner than anyone else. The longer you wait on that, the longer the shooter has to kill unopposed.

Also, there are circumstances where even though willing, you would not seek out an engagement. If you have family with you when the shooting starts, your first duty is to see them safe. There will be exceptions to even this, of course. Little if anything about this is hard and fast or black and white. Understand that too.

Just do think about this ahead of time. It is important.

Check your weapons.

- High-capacity (as high as the law allows, at least).
- Magazine-fed.
- Semi-auto.
- 9mm/.38 Super caliber or higher.
- One reload for that at the minimum. (More if you're in a capacity-limited area.)

That is the minimum I recommend and the minimum I believe anyone who carries should leave their home with. There are those that for various reasons (physical disability or lack of strength, for example) cannot handle larger caliber weapons or manipulate semi-autos with facility—they should carry what they can shoot accurately. If you're not a member of that group however, leave the J-frame and the pocket-sized .380 at home or carry it only as a backup to the larger pistol.

This recommendation is for general carry and not just in case you have to face an active shooter, but here I will limit the reasons for this recommendation to those most applicable to an active-shooter situation:

- Higher capacity in-gun and faster reloads—you can stay in the fight longer without a pause. Even with a single shooter, the fight could easily go longer than the average self-defense encounter. If there are multiple shooters, you could either be engaged for a long time (relatively speaking) or go through a series of shorter engagements over time if you are able to isolate smaller elements of the group (Even if escaping, which is recommended in a multiple-shooter attack, you must be prepared to fight someone on the way out.). That argues for the ability to keep shooting and to be able to get the gun back "up" in the very shortest amount of time. Revolvers don't make it on either of those criteria.

- Better sights and more power at longer ranges—there is an increased chance that you will chose to or be forced to engage an active shooter beyond the limits of the average self-defense encounter. To have the best chance of stopping the killing as soon as possible, you need accuracy and power beyond the 3, 5, 10, 15, even 25-yard limits that most defensive shooters think of fighting at. Several recent encounters could have been ended more quickly if someone had engaged shooters who were more than 20 yards away. While you want to be as close as possible to take the decisive shot, a good set-up with a rest farther away can be a surer thing than any unsupported closer position when the rounds are or may be going both ways. Furthermore, you will want a round that will do damage out to as far as you can get a hit with. You can make the shot with a snub-nose revolver, yes. You can do damage over many yards with a .380, yes. What you can do is going to be less than what you want to do when you're trying to neutralize somebody down the hall with a rifle in their hands.

What you want then is what I'll call at least a "fifty-yard gun"—something that combines the sights, the trigger, the solidity and weight, and the weight of fire that smaller and smaller-capacity weapons cannot muster. Is that what you're carrying? If not, why are you limiting yourself and your options?

Check your supporting gear.

There's more to a 'fighting pistol' than just the pistol. We sometimes making the mistake of not thinking what else has to go with that pistol to make us more fully able to respond to a sudden attack. To properly do that we need to embrace the concept of the 'weapon system' like the military does.

A weapon system includes the weapon itself and everything that is required to keep it running reliably, get it to a battlefield in condition to fire as soon as it's needed, and to support it in position for as long as necessary. To take an artillery missile system as an example, you need the missile itself, a launcher for it, a transporter for that launcher, tools and parts to keep the missile and launcher ready to fire the missile with, aiming and fire-direction systems that enable the missile to hit its target, and reloads for the launcher so that the system can continue to fire as long as needed, among other things.

In the same way, a fighting pistol also needs some supporting elements. A holster of good quality and a good belt to carry that holster on for transport and storage on your person; one or more reloads so that you can if needed continue to shoot; lubricants and cleaners to maintain the pistol in operating condition; spare parts so that you can replace anything worn or worn down to keep the pistol ready for immediate use; sights or optics to allow for good aiming and precision when shooting. These and other things are all part of the system that supports you and your weapon and keeps it ready and able to function at the moment of need. Paying attention to the whole system (which includes your own training and maintenance of skill with the weapon) instead of thinking the gun is all there is could mean the difference between winning or losing and living or dying if you're there when the shooting starts.

Besides the weapon system, other supporting equipment should be considered for inclusion in your everyday carry (EDC) inventory. A flashlight is one of these items. Lighted buildings don't always stay lighted. A sufficiently powerful light can be used to distract an attacker to give you an additional moment to take action. It can also be used as a striking tool with the advantage that you can carry a flashlight in places that don't allow you to carry weapons. Even if you are one of those who has a light on their EDC weapon—maybe especially if you do—a separate flashlight can still be very handy exactly because it can be used separately from the weapon.

A good knife is also recommended as a part of your EDC setup. Whether you decide on a knife specifically meant to fight with or just a general-purpose blade that might be used to fight with, even a small knife can be handy at times other than during an attack and during emergencies that don't involve any exchange of blows or gunfire. A (relatively) large fixed-blade knife (if laws where you live allow such things to be kept and carried) is preferable but even a small knife can do damage as long as you pick your targets and commit to the attack. If you carry a knife with the idea that you will fight with it, do spend some time practicing your access of the blade so that it is as safe, sure, and quick as possible when it has to be. And seek training on how to fight with a knife (and against one). If the knife is not an option for self-defense, give thought to how to use something like an ordinary pen or pencil as a stand-in stabbing weapon. You don't need to get one of the many "tactical" pens that are marketed for use as counter-offensive weapons to have something you can do damage with. As long as you know how to use it in a pinch and can commit fully to doing damage with it, almost any pen or pencil will give you at least one good strike.

The next thing I recommend that you consider keeping with you at all times is a basic medical kit with contents selected to let you deal with at least one penetrating wound such as a gunshot wound. A good-quality tourniquet, a large bandage or wrap, a way to secure the bandage or wrap, and possibly some form of blood-stopper/clotting agent is the minimum I would recommend for such a kit. A pair of surgical/medical gloves and a small pair of scissors to cut away clothing with will not take up much more space, nor will a small roll of wide tape. This and the knowledge of how to use it, added to the knowledge and ability to improvise bindings and tourniquets from clothing or other items that may be at hand, will allow you to help the victims of an active shooter survive until professional medical personnel have been cleared to enter the area of the attack. Perhaps more importantly, it can be the difference between you being able to keep yourself going so you can stop the attack or being disabled and killed or left to see others die if you get hit yourself.

This kind of kit will not take up much space if properly packed. Pre-made kits can fit in a large pocket, in a small pack not much bigger than a large smartphone on the belt, on wrapped around the ankle and covered by a pants-leg. There are many schools and instructors that will provide extensive training on what to do with these tools and how to do it. Check the References section of this book for a few sources for that training and information. A larger kit with additional items and/or extras of the items in your personal kit could be carried in a bag or backpack to further extend the capabilities of the personal kit. But even if you do keep a bag of some kind with you or nearby as a rule or habit, I recommend you keep a minimal set of wound-treatment gear on your body.

If you do carry a bag of some type, consider the addition of an armor plate rated to at least level IIIA in it. The same kind of plates that are carried in vests to protect police and military personnel will fit in even small bags and can add an additional level of protection if you ever have to confront an active shooter or protect someone that might be targeted by one. Some countries and some parts of countries may prohibit the personal ownership of armor like this, but if it is legal to have it, modern plate armor is not as much additional weight or mass as it used to be, and Level IIIA or IV armor will stop even repeated hits from rifles of the type most likely to be carried by an active shooter. And it could provide the edge you need to win or escape unharmed in an emergency.

Prepare yourself.

Some people still think that if you carry a gun you don't have to be in shape to fight. You just need enough strength to hold it steady and pull the trigger, right?

Believing that is a good way to set yourself up to die in any fight, not just this one. Consider this:

You will be under stress. Your body will be dumping chemicals into your system, some of them pretty strong ones. You will be going through the "fight or flight" physiological and neurochemical ramp-up. And that's just if you're standing still listening to the gunfire after you realize what is happening. That helps you if you have to or decide to fight or fly, but it takes a physical toll from you in the process. Good physical condition helps you deal with that. If you're in sight of the shooter, you will be taking fire or somewhere on the list of imminent targets. Time to go, go, go. Evasive movement, displacement to cover or concealment, movement to or away from the shooter is what you will need to do and keep doing for a while.

Good physical condition allows you to move quicker, go faster, and keep going longer when you have to do that.

You won't be alone, either. If you're by yourself, you'll have to work through or around everybody that's running away trying to escape or hide. Now add family you're trying to guide, push, pull or carry to safety. Whether you're working your way toward or away from the shooter, you have to run the stream of panicked people, protect your weapon, shelter and guide those who are with you, avoid being knocked about and/or trampled. Good physical condition lets you ward off others, keep your feet, and physically move others as you need to.

Even if you're in the clear where others are concerned, you are likely to be moving either to escape or engage the shooter(s). You will want to be ready for a sudden encounter while you're doing that, and you want to move in such a way as to minimize your exposure and maximize your chances of seeing the shooter(s) before they see you. Those of you who have fought in or gone through buildings that might have threats in them know what kind of movement I'm talking about. Those of you who have paid much attention to videos of building entries and room-to-room searches and fighting have an idea about it. It's not a hard thing to learn, moving like you need to, but even in the relatively open spaces of an office building or mall it's still going to be a physical drain on you. And don't forget the biochemical mix your body has flowing through you. Moving through a building ready to fight if you have to, or looking for a fight—also called Close-Quarter Battle or "tactical" movement—is not just an adventure, it is a job. Good conditioning lets you keep it up longer and do it easier and leaves you more to fight with, if that's what you end up doing at some point.

Good conditioning helps you think things through, keep a clear head and your confidence up for however long the fight lasts. It's harder to come up when a plan when your body is demanding air and your muscles are burning from fatigue. The longer you can delay that, and the faster you can recover from that when it happens, the better you can plot and plan and consider. Physical condition affects mental condition. The better the one, the better the other.

Besides the body, the mind must be prepared as well. Part of this is assuming the attitude necessary to this fight, which has been discussed. Besides that, knowledge of strategy and tactics, knowledge of use of weapons, knowledge of how to use what is available to best advantage, knowledge of the potential threat and the characteristics of it will all be useful, not just for this fight but for many others you may face. Learning how to move safely and fight effectively through a group of boutique stores in a shopping center also teaches you how to move safely and fight effectively against a home invader. Learning how to fight with a gun works for you whether it's against an active shooter in an office building or an armed robber in a parking lot. To prepare for any possible fight, much less this one, think, study, train, consider. This does not require immense resources or the dedication of a monk. It does require a commitment to be better than you are now, to know more than you do now, to spend some time on a regular and/or ongoing basis to make yourself better able to fight for those you love and who love you.

And it will benefit you even if you never have to fight. What's not to like about that?

Map the battlefield.

This can be considered a part of preparing yourself for a fight or done as a separate issue. What I mean by mapping the battlefield is getting into the habit of looking over the terrain wherever you are and taking a little time to consider how it would affect your ability to fight.

Terrain is everywhere. It is not just limited to open fields, hills and valleys, roads and rivers. The cluster of cubicles on one floor of an office building is terrain. The counter area of a fast food store is terrain. The main concourse of a shopping mall is terrain. All of it has places where you can move better in some directions than others, hidden and open spaces, elevations and depressions, barriers to movement and vision, and other features that can work for or against you when confronted by an active shooter (or other criminal attack).

The study of the terrain you live and work in goes beyond the idea of knowing where the entrances and exits are and where to sit so your back is covered and you can see around you. How can you use counters, shelving units, racks, stacked merchandise, walls and halls to help you defeat an attack? How can it be used to defeat you? Where is the open field, the choke point, the hard point, the line of sight, in the grocery store? Where can you ambush and be ambushed in an office building? It doesn't take as much time and effort as you might think to begin thinking in these terms. It does take an awareness that there is more to where you are than walls and halls, furniture, parked cars and traffic lanes. But the time you spend now, looking at it as if you were plotting a battle about to take place there, could be worth more than you imagine in the moment when, without warning, life is on the line.

Run some simulations.

This is useful enough outside of fight preparation, and important enough within it, that I consider it worth a separate section. Simulations in this context are "mind fights" that you can run nearly any time. The amount of detail and level of intensity you can generate are limited only by your imagination and your ability to tune out what is happening around you.

Simulations vary in detail from simple what-ifs that can be thought about during idle moments, much like a focused daydream, all the way up to dedicated visualization that involves enough focus that you would jump if someone touched you while you're were running through one. All of it at every level can be useful for everything from the practice of a specific skill (playing a piece of music on a mental piano; practicing a golf swing; going through handgun malfunction-correction or reloading techniques) to the study of a full-on scenario (meat counter of the grocery store hearing gunshots and screams from the area of the cash register) and all manner of things in between those.

Focused visualization has been used as a development tool by elite athletes and as a means of staying sane by prisoners of war. It has been proven effective as a means of skill development by scientific studies and actual experience. It provides both a means of training for scenarios and events that otherwise require much expense and great effort to set up in reality, and as a means of programming yourself to not be totally surprised by sudden or life-threatening events. Visualization can be a primary mechanism in limiting the risk that we will panic and react the wrong way when faced with an unexpected event. Properly focused and structured visualization can provide the primitive "fight or flight" functions of our brain with something it has "seen" before that is near to what it sees now. The more unknown a situation is, the more unfamiliar something is, the more likely that our primitive brain will trigger an incorrect reaction or even freeze us up completely. Visualization provides us the ability to familiarize our minds and emotions with things we cannot otherwise experience in reality. The primitive mind doesn't know the difference between real experience and proper visualization and so takes what is familiar and doesn't fall prey to panic and the resulting indecision or wrong decision-making that goes with it.

Visualization is a useful tool in your defensive training box and too useful to you to ignore its ongoing use. Make it a part of your preparation for defense against all kinds of attack. Maintain your mind like you maintain your weapon. Condition your mind like you condition your body. Train your mind like you train yourself to shoot. On the day when it all has to come together, you will be glad you did.

Modifying the Carry Gun

There are some things you can change on your carry gun that could help you end an active shooter incident more quickly. The longer anyone is shooting in such an incident the more likely that someone other than the attacker will get hit. Stopping the attack quickly makes everyone safer. Some modifications you can make or have done by a gunsmith could help you do that.

Most of the modifications considered here are meant to increase the accuracy of the weapon. Since there is a higher likelihood that range to an active shooter will be longer than is normal for most self-defense shootings and that shooting for CNS is more often recommended in these cases, greater mechanical accuracy will be helpful as long as you have the capability to make use of it.

Two caveats:

- **NO MODIFICATION SHOULD BE ALLOWED TO AFFECT RELIABILITY**. If the gun doesn't function or stops functioning during the fight it doesn't matter how much more accurate it is or what a modification could do for you if it were working. Dead guns could mean a dead you in a hurry. If a change from stock affects reliability of operation of your carry weapon don't even think about making it.

- **If you don't put the work in then money on modifications is wasted and useless.** Gadgets do not infuse skill when they are installed. Understand that most guns are more accurate than you are right out of the box. Until you start to match the accuracy of a stock gun it is probably a waste of time and money to make a modification.

Suggested add-ons and modifications include but are not limited to:

- <u>Replacement sights</u> – Stock sights on most pistols are made for the average counteroffensive shooter to fight under the most common circumstances—a reactive fight at close range. And while there are many shooters who are very, very accurate indeed with stock sights, most can and do find improvement by replacing those with aftermarket versions optimized for high visibility, precision shooting, or both.

- <u>Trigger modifications</u> – Modifications to the trigger to improve function and enhance accuracy and control are not limited to reducing the weight of the trigger pull. Smoothing and polishing the action or, where such is available, replacing the stock curved trigger with a flat-faced trigger (several companies make flat triggers for Glocks to cite a common example) can increase accuracy without changing anything else about the trigger mechanism. Some shooters will do better with a modest reduction in trigger pull, yes, but a decision to so alter the trigger of any weapon you may use in a fight must be done only after very careful consideration.
    - Trigger modifications should be intended to increase accuracy as a way to end a violent attack as soon as possible while keeping reliability of operation. The faster and better you hit, the fewer shots anyone in the fight will fire or have to fire. That makes it safer for everyone,

fighting or not. For a fighting gun in any role that should be the primary goal of any modification, trigger or other part. If an add-on or modification is not going to help you fight better, it should not be made. Where trigger weight modifications are concerned, while everyone can benefit from polishing and smoothing not everyone will benefit from reduction in trigger weight of pull. So think about that specific step before you commit to it.
  - (Frankly speaking, I believe the majority of those that carry concealed should not do anything that reduces the trigger pull weight from the stock setting on their pistol. This is one case where you should put a lot of time learning to be good with what you have before you change anything about that aspect of it.)

- <u>Optics, mainly red-dot sights</u> – It may take some time and work to adjust to one but once you have a red-dot sight on a handgun can make long and precision shots easier and get you on target more quickly that standard sights. The current drawback to them is cost—quality sights suitable for use on a fighting handgun start at 400 dollars and most are nearer to 500.
  - It is hard to argue against the idea of mounting a red-dot on a combat handgun now that HK, Smith and Wesson and Glock all offer handguns that can be fitted with dot-sights for sale in the US. Dot-sights, mounted directly to the slide or on an adapter, may not be a given individual's cup of tea but the general market, including military and police special-operations units and private contractor groups have examined the concept and found it Good. And the handgun red-dot has been proven in combat now. So the question is not is adding one useful, but if adding one will give you enough extra

capability to justify the price of the mount and the sight itself.
    - If you are going to add a dot-sight to a gun meant to be a fighting weapon I recommend you pay the extra money to have the slide milled specifically for your chosen sight. The multi-sight mounts offered on retail guns are reported to have problems and not be reliable enough for me to suggest you go with a pre-cut option such as is currently offered.
    - Also, make sure you have back-up sights (suppressor sights are most common as they allow sighting through the glass of the dot-sight) mounted in addition to the dot and that you are going to put in the work required to fully adjust to the dot-sight. Make it or any other add-on or modification you make to any gun a useful piece of equipment and not just another gadget.
- <u>Match-grade barrels</u> – It is entirely possible, perhaps likely, that you will have enough time in an active shooter event to set up your shot. Also, consider the increased likelihood that you will be shooting at beyond-normal encounter ranges and at smaller targets (either because of range or the need to target CNS for the fastest stop). Given those factors, replacing the stock barrel with a match-grade barrel is not a bad idea <u>as long as it does not affect reliability</u>. All the additional capability in the world is useless to you if you can't depend on it working when you need it. As long as it still works reliably with the more accurate barrel, though, swapping out that stock component is something you may want to consider as a modification to your carry weapon.
- <u>Lasers</u> – If you have a red-dot or other optic it is probably not necessary. Otherwise it might be helpful to have one to make it easier to set up a longer-range or precision shot. If you do decide to add a laser I recommend you get a green laser to provide for greater range and visibility in daylight or lighted areas. And make sure you train enough with the laser to avoid the possibly-fatal tendency to chase the dot (

- Practice target-focused snap-shots, drawing from the holster and going to first an eight-inch area at close range, progressing to a four-inch circle from farther away. Train so that you do <u>not</u> wait until the dot is on a precise point to shoot when you have to shoot quickly. Save that focus for precision shots when you have time.). Also, make sure you are aware of how the laser points back at you when you use it and plan for that eventuality. (Especially when the other guy has a rifle. attracting fire is not a desirable outcome of laser-sight employment.)

Again: Think carefully about any modification you make to your carry gun before you make it. If you cannot justify that modification to an investigator after a shooting incident on grounds that it made you able to end the fight and stop the attack more quickly and effectively, then don't make it. And don't make a modification unless you are prepared to put in the work to make sure you get the best possible performance out of that change.

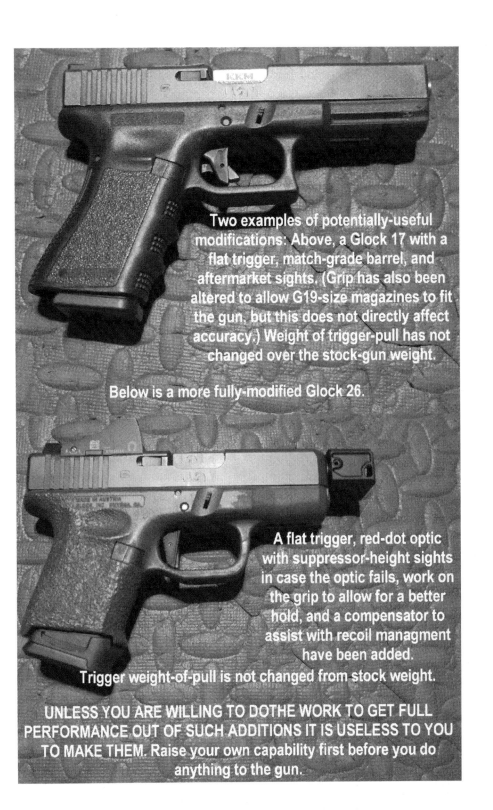

Targeting the Head

Starting somewhere around the time of the Brussels attack the idea of going immediately for a head shot (instead of hitting Center Of Mass and targeting the attacker's the head only if that did not effect a stop) started being brought up on some online forums and other discussion and opinion venues. After the Istanbul attack that idea began moving into forums populated by more 'casual' gun carriers, those who up to then still considered a five-shot revolver or a .380 pocket pistol as adequate for all their defensive needs.

Now (at the time of this writing) we have the assault on and killing and wounding of members of the Dallas police department by a man wearing body armor that stopped otherwise-fatal pistol hits one officer made on him. (There was another incident of an armor-wearer shooting police officers a few weeks after the Dallas incident.) Besides that, chest rigs and vests full of spare magazines that some active shooters have worn could slow down a pistol bullet enough that it doesn't penetrate to a vital organ. In an ad-hoc test I conducted in 2016 I saw 9mm hollow-point rounds stopped completely by loaded AK-47 magazines. Load-bearing gear and equipment on it is not the same as body armor but could be a factor affecting our ability to stop the attack, and so it should be taken into account in our thinking and planning. It is now surely time to consider reasons, ways and means of targeting the attacker's mind so that they can be stopped as near to instantly as possible.

Consider first the structure of the head and placement of the brain and other organs of control of the body in it. Not all targets on and in the head are equal if you want the best chance of an instant stop from your shot. The brain itself is one of the best-protected organs in the body. Pistol rounds have skipped off the skull without penetrating or gone around from one side of the head to the other underneath the skin covering the skull. Besides that the organ that when hit will shut down the attacker the way a light switch turns off a light—what is called the no-reflex point—is not in the brain but at the base of it. For best effect and the best chance of an immediate stop to the attack, then, you want to target an area in the lower half of the head and more specifically in a band one to one-and-a-half inches wide centered approximately at the base of the nose in front.

Desirable target points are: From the front, the base or tip of the nose; from the side, the ear canal or earlobe; and from the back, the line made by the hinges of the jaw at the base of the skull where head meets neck. Put hits on these places and you have a good chance of removing the attacker's ability to pull a trigger or flip a switch on a bomb.

Practically speaking a solid hit anywhere on the head, whether inside this band or not, will probably disrupt or stop the attack, at least long enough to set up a better follow-up shot. But people have been shot in the head and still were able to (and did) continue fighting. And if they have a finger on a trigger or a switch or button the flinch reaction from a general-area hit might cause a shot to go off or the switch or button to be flipped or pressed even if it kills them. That outcome should be avoided if it is at all possible to do it.

But such a shot may require more precision than some of us are currently capable of producing. Any shooter thinking about putting a priority on targeting the head has to be as honest as they can be about what they can do right now. If you can't place or keep a shot within a 3" x 5" index card or 4"-5" circle reliably you probably should not consider shooting for the head. (Besides their use as a baseline accuracy index, you can also use those targets to get an idea of limit of range at which you have a good chance of making that head shot.)

Understand that I am not recommending or asking you to consider a head shot under any and all circumstances. Reacting to the close-range appearance of an active shooter when the priority is not being hit, getting your weapon out and lined up and getting hits RIGHT NOW is not a situation where I suggest you try lining up on the base of the brain. Though there are some who can move evasively and get that kind of shooting done, the majority of us, I dare say, cannot and should not try. The situation and circumstances must dictate the technique(s) and tactic(s) used. You should not attempt to pound the square peg into the round hole once the fight is on.

What I'm suggesting, and what you will see suggested in the outline portion of this book, is a shot from ambush, preferably using a supported position like the ones you see in the Examples section. Get to the side or behind the active shooter, set up, and take a shot aimed as carefully as possible to the center of the head inside the band described earlier. That will give you the best chance of shutting the attacker down and ending the killing quickly.

To have the best chance of doing this when you're under the stress of attack, start practicing and training on small targets. Don't be satisfied any longer with keeping shots inside an eight-inch pie plate or the A-zone of an IDPA target. Start in close with a four-inch circle and go back as far as you can with it. Then go back in close and do it again with a two-inch circle. Then a one-inch circle. Then a dot. Start at five yards each time. Backing it out three to five yards at a time, see if you can go out to fifty yards (the circles and dots will, by necessity, have to be bigger at that range, but don't go over three inches in diameter). Don't apply any constraints to yourself initially except the requirement for accuracy. Once you get that, you can add something like a timer and start working on the speed of the accurate shot, working close-to-far again. If you make that two-inch circle at fifty yards, consider adding some kind of physical stress to the shooting exercise starting back at five yards again.

That way when the threat is real and the stress hits you and you're lining up that shot, you won't have to worry as much about keeping it on.

And you'll know when you're too far away to have a chance and need to find another place to shoot from (if you're committed to the shot). The less you have to worry and distract you, the better you can think. The better you can think, the more likely you can stay alive.

Also, think about setting up the shot to the head by a shot or shots to another part of the body. Even if they do have a bomb vest or armor on, those will not cover everything. The lower torso at the belt line and below—the pelvic region—will probably not be covered. Neither with the arms or legs. And it may be that your position doesn't give you a head shot but it does give you another part of the body. Taking the target you have is likely to slow the attacker down and distract them and may even stop them from shooting more. That pause or partial stop will make it easier to line up the shot to the head that ends the attack. Keep this kind of preparatory shot in mind.

Also: If the attacker has or you suspect they have a bomb vest and you have brought them down without killing them, you need to shoot them in the head to prevent them from triggering the bomb. It is the same as you shooting a downed attacker who is moving toward or who is still trying to raise a gun up to shoot you even though they are down. Either one poses a deadly threat to you and everyone around you and must be stopped. Especially with a bomber, there must be no hesitation about this. Down or not, you must make sure they cannot move at all.

These are some of the factors and considerations I think you should know about when preparing to target the head.

Vehicles

Vehicles ranging from small cars to eighteen-wheelers have been used in attacks. As of the time of this is written, the tendency appears to be that smaller vehicles are used both as weapons in their own right and as transports for the attacker(s), while larger vehicles are the primary killing tool used in the attack. So we need to have or get some understanding of how to deal, in one way or another, with a vehicular assault, whether that is just the initial stage of an attack or the attack itself.

You want to think about two things: Not being hit by the vehicle, and stopping the vehicle. Let's consider not being hit first.

Attacks so far have occurred on streets and (in at least one case) bridges. These are all narrow areas where targets for the driver are nominally crowded together but all of them so far also offer enough room to evade the oncoming vehicle. On most streets, buildings, other cars parked or stopped, and fixtures like light and power poles and street signs are close enough to reach and get behind as long as you have even a little warning time. And while a pole or even another vehicle or building front won't necessarily stop the attacking vehicle immediately, it is unlikely they will try and go through it when they can continue along the open street after others who have not gotten away.

Even if such cover or other obstacles are not available it is still possible to get out of the way of an oncoming vehicle as long as you don't panic. Remember that especially large and heavy vehicles can't move directly to the side like you can. Keep your wits about you, time the approach as best you can, and move suddenly and quickly directly to the side or at a forward angle. Even allowing for some leeway about the timing of your move, you can likely get to the side and well inside of the turning radius of the car or truck before it hits. You only need to move a few feet to cause it to miss you, remember.

Stopping a vehicle before it hits you or goes on to hit someone else is not as easy as some would have you believe it is, but even if you can evade it I believe it is an attempt worth making even if it fails. It may not be easy to stop a car or truck, especially a big one, with just your handgun but it can be done. And I think it better to try and fail in the attempt than to let them go on and run down anyone else.

The fastest way to stop the vehicle is to stop the driver. That's what is said and it's true. But it's not as simple and easy as that line of advice might imply, either. From the front the driver is protected by the laminated, angled and curved front windshield glass and, in most vehicles, by the engine. The front windshield is not bulletproof but the combination of lamination, angling, and curvature makes it resistant enough to gunfire to think of it as light armor plate. Handgun rounds especially have been deflected or even stopped by front windshield glass—though it is unlikely to happen if you are using a caliber of at least 9mm Luger or .38 Super or higher—and the material of the windshield will change the direction of rounds that penetrate it. This changes the POA/POI (Point Of Aim/Point Of Impact) relationship a bit. Shots fired from outside tend to hit below the point of aim of the one shooting. For that reason some will advise you to aim a little higher than normal when shooting into a vehicle through the front glass.

You should ignore that advice. Here's why:

If you're ever in front of an oncoming car you will be under considerable stress already to say the least. Add to that the fact that very few if any of us have ever had the opportunity to shoot through a windshield to see how the bullets fired will travel after they've gone through. Add to <u>that</u> the fact that most of those test-firing opportunities occur at closer distances than we want to be in front of a moving vehicle before we should start moving out of the way of it. Few if any of us will be able to adjust enough to place the shots in the same way we would if there was not angled, curved, and laminated glass between us and the target. The chance that we would over-correct and either miss entirely or have the bullets deflected by the angled glass combining with a small upward angle of an over-corrected aim is too high.

    Sight the same way you always do on the upper body or head of the driver and start shooting. A lot. Make a hole in the glass and put more rounds through that hole. Empty the magazine and get out of the way as you reload if you have time. Continue shooting as the vehicle passes you if it is still moving.

    Do understand that you will still have to get out of the way whether you stop the driver or not. Because stopping the driver still doesn't stop the vehicle. There's not an engine kill switch wired to the driver's heart or brain. Killing the driver may take pressure off the accelerator or not. The vehicle may coast to a stop or not. It may veer off the line it's on and go another direction and crash into something or not. You need to be aware of this and make sure you're not where it goes before it finally does stop.

    If you're not in front, you'll be taking your shots at the driver from the side or behind. From directly behind you aim exactly as you do from the front. The good news here is that the rear windshield is not laminated and won't deflect the bullet(s) like the front does. And if you choose or have to go lower than the windshield there is far less from behind that will stop a bullet going through if there is anything at all. And shots that miss the driver are less likely to continue out in the same line and possibly strike someone in front of the vehicle especially if you're aiming below the line of the head. (What's on the far side of the target needs to be considered if it is at all possible. You can't ignore that consideration without very, <u>very</u> good reasons why you are doing that.) BUT, you may not want to go lower in your targeting for two reasons: Hits to the lower torso may not stop the driver from being able to drive, and the car may contain explosives or flammable substances that would be hit and maybe set off if you target lower than you do from the front.

From the side the good news is that once again you're not firing through curved, angled, and laminated glass and that little if anything in the door of the vehicle will stop even a handgun round. The bad news is that you'll be trying a crossing shot at what is probably going to be a pretty fast-moving target. The possible variances of angle and speed and target area or point is much too wide for me to offer specific advice to you about that. All I can say is that if you're confident you can make the crossing shot, make the crossing shot. (Again, considering what or who is on the opposite side that might be in danger from a missed shot.) Otherwise it is probably better to let the vehicle pass and then get directly behind it before you shoot.

If the vehicle does stop, either because you stopped the driver or because it was stopped by something, stay ready in case someone in the car comes out to continue the attack. This has happened in Europe. Be aware that the vehicle is not only weapon, it is also a transport, and act accordingly.

If you cannot stop the driver then stopping the vehicle becomes a <u>lot</u> harder, especially with just the handgun you are most likely to have on you at the time of the attack. It's not impossible and I for one believe it should be attempted if that's all you can do, but I don't want to give you false hope that a well-placed shot or shots is going to kill the engine or prevent the vehicle from going on for a long time. Historical examples indicate that getting even a small car to stop quickly from damage isn't going to happen if you're hitting it with anything less than a 12ga shotgun slug or a .50 caliber rifle. Don't let it stop you from trying but at the same time don't expect it to work. And do make sure you're not in the path of the vehicle while you're trying.

The other thing to be wary of with a vehicle is the possibility of it carrying explosives or flammables. For that reason, I recommend that you not approach the vehicle where it stops. You should, in fact, seek distance and cover in case there is an explosive device inside. Refer to the chapter 'Bombs' for more information about that possibility.

Engaging from the front, you have to judge at what point you have a good chance of hitting the part of the driver that is most exposed against the time and distance you need to be sure of getting out of the way of the oncoming vehicle.

The available target area is small and you should assume that your first shot (perhaps even the first two or three) will be expended breaking through the front windshield laminate.

You will not have long to set yourself, aim, and fire before you have to move. Be prepared to make the most of the opportunity while you have it.

Don't wait too long to move to the side and prepare to make a crossing shot as the vehicle passes.

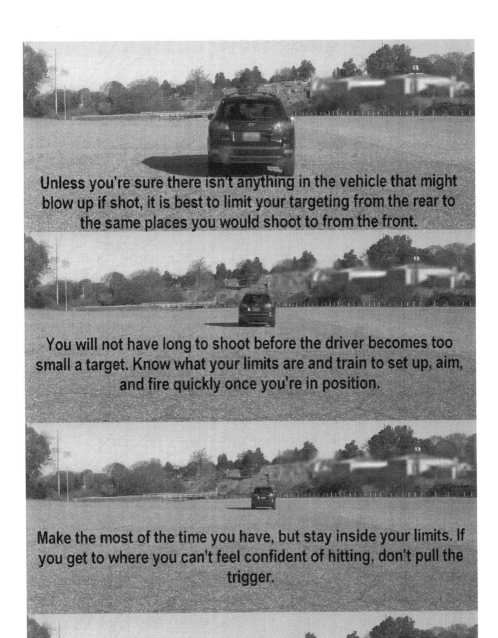

Blades

Attacks with blades (usually knives but machetes and axes have also been used) are more common in Europe but have also occurred in the US. A blade of some type might be used in cases where the attacker cannot access a firearm either as quickly as they want to act or where they are unaware of extra-legal ways to obtain a gun. There is also the possibility that the blade is chosen because the attacker wants to make a close personal strike on the chosen target(s) and/or a certain kind of statement that an attack with a gun or bomb does not make.

Whatever the reason a bladed weapon is resorted to, you want to be aware of the possibility that it may be a knife or an axe and not a gun that is directed at you or someone else. And you need at least a basic understanding of how to deal with it.

Besides that, you may find yourself in a place or environment where your only weapon might be a knife or an improvised stabbing weapon of some type. Even a basic idea of how to use that to best effect against an active shooter could one day be very useful indeed. So both defense and offense will be briefly considered in this chapter.

The nature of the blade attack I am discussing here is different from the way a criminal is likely to use a knife. A criminal will attempt to bring the blade as close to you as possible before they use it. They will want to provide you as little warning as possible before they act. Also, the blade may not be used to kill as often as it is used as a tool of intimidation, something to give the criminal more control of the situation and a better chance to get what he wants from you without risk. If killing is the aim of the criminal there is a good chance that you will not know the knife is there until you are struck with it, and perhaps not even then.

The terrorist or disturbed person attacking with a blade may make more of a display of it as they attack unless 1) you are the first target chosen and 2) you are in a confined space such as a train or subway car or in a dense crowd of people. For the terrorist, the attack is intended as a message and display as much as it is to kill. They will want others to know and be afraid of what they are doing and can do. There are also cases where an attack begins in one way—a vehicular attack, for example—and then is continued using a blade of some type.

A disturbed person may not be enough in control of themselves to go quietly about their killing. In each of these cases you are more (perhaps not much more, but somewhat more at least) to have some warning of the attack either by their (perhaps inadvertent) declaration of intent or by their attack on someone else nearby.

When You're Defending.

What too many gun-carriers don't understand enough is that dealing with a blade attack is not always and only just a matter of drawing their gun and shooting the attacker. Circumstances of the attack can easily favor the knife-wielder and there have been cases where having a gun did not prevent a person from being stabbed or hacked to death. The first step in dealing with a blade attack as a gun-carrier is that <u>you must acknowledge that the gun does not trump all other weapons every time no matter what</u>. The second step is understanding what you have to do in some cases to get to where it is safe to draw your gun so that you can use it to stop someone from attacking with a different weapon.

We'll consider knives first, as they are the most common contact weapon used in mass attacks.

Distance usually defines the nature of the problem.

The primary criteria for knowing you can 'go to guns' immediately is the knowledge that the knife is in play and the distance from you to the knife-wielder. Even if they're far enough away that you have time to get the gun on-line, surprise can give them enough time to get too close for you to make it a 'gun problem' from the get-go. If they start the attack within a certain distance from you, unless you know it's coming at least two or three seconds ahead of time there will be no time for you to get to your gun. You have to deal with the knife attack first with the aim of getting time and space to make it a gun problem.

About the term 'gun problem': The phrase 'When all you have is a hammer, everything looks like a nail' is repeated with good reason and is entirely too applicable to the common concealed-weapon carrier. It's not all their fault that it is, either. Once we decide to seek training that's the weapon we train with and the object of our focus. We train to act and react with the gun, only the gun, and nothing but the gun so much that we inadvertently program ourselves to look at any and every attack first as a gun problem that can and will be solved by the introduction of the gun. The amount of time we spend in training covering critical distance and the importance of that concept when dealing with contact weapons like knives or clubs is trivial compared to the time we spend dealing with what are clearly gun problems that occur at gun-problem distances. So we inadvertently condition ourselves to think of any attack as a 'gun problem' even when it is not.

That conditioning is what may get us killed in the event someone pulls a knife on us.

It's important to keep in mind that trying to draw your gun in immediate response to a close-distance attack is not the most useful and life-saving response. It's important to, as much as you can, be able to respond without the gun and without needing the gun immediately to defend yourself. As much as you can you need at least some basic empty-hand and improvised-weapon skill and knowledge and be in good enough physical condition (as good as is possible given your personal circumstances) so that you can keep yourself alive and get yourself to a position where you can go to your gun. Empty-hand combat skills and ability to move evasively come into their own in those first instances when the knifer is inside of the critical distance where the gun can't be put into action.

Critical Distance.

What is that critical distance? The rule of thumb is twenty-one feet. That's seven yards or not quite six and a half meters and it seems like a longer distance than it is until you have seen it demonstrated. In reality I assign no less than thirty feet—ten yards or a little over nine meters—as critical distance, and make the same recommendation to you. Between about thirty feet and about fifteen feet, evasive movement is key. You have to be able to get off the line of the knifer's advance at the same time as you are drawing your gun.

Move, preferably to the side or flank (backing straight up is the least desirable option; don't go backwards unless you can't go any other way to change distance and positional relationship) and keep moving. If the knifer is committed to their attack, their adjustment to your movement will be slower than your re-positioning and presentation and you will be able to engage without having to make contact. Don't try to stand there and out-draw the rush. It is unlikely you will manage it. Even if you get hits on the attacker they will likely live long enough to close in and stab you repeatedly. This is not a sporting contest and you don't want to try to live with a tie. You want a clear and decisive victory. Movement is what gets you that.

If the attacker starts inside of fifteen feet of distance and especially if they're within ten feet, give up the idea of getting the gun out and go with empty-hands and/or improvised weapons to resist the initial part of the attack. The goal here is to prevent stabs or slashes to vital areas of the body and head and to change position and distance. Doing damage to the attacker while you do this is desirable but not necessary IF you can get clear enough and time enough so that you can get your gun into action.

Understand that you must commit all of your effort and resources into the physical defense during the first seconds. Forget the common instruction that has you offering a defense with one arm while you draw the gun with the other one. A committed attacker can blow through that and kill you. <u>It is not a gun problem yet.</u> <u>You have to make it a gun problem by solving the unarmed-defense problem first</u>. Half measures like the commonly-recommended defensive techniques will not keep you alive. Defend yourself from the knife <u>first</u>. Once that is done and you have created time and distance by the unarmed defensive response, then and only then should you go to guns for final resolution if that is still required.

Another thing to understand about defending yourself inside of critical distance is that you don't have to get yourself outside of critical distance to get to your gun <u>if</u> you can manage your position in relation to the attacker the right way. By moving and re-directing, you can place yourself on the flank or even behind the attacker and give yourself enough time to draw the gun and engage even if you are still inside of the thirty-foot line. See the photo section for examples of ways to do this.

You want also to be able to accept the fact that you will probably get cut. If the knifer starts within ten feet and targets you, you might well be stabbed or slashed before you know you're under attack. And you might not know you've been stabbed or slashed immediately, either. You might not feel anything but the physical impact(s) first. Victims of knife attacks have repeatedly reported this and it's something you need to both understand and come to terms with.

At these close and very-close distances your goals have to be limited. Forget trying to grapple, forget trying to disarm the knife, forget what you've seen in movies and martial arts demonstrations and maybe even what you've been taught in self-defense class. You want to avoid getting crippling damage or injury and you want to get away from the knife far enough and long enough that you can either completely escape or draw your gun and engage the knifer. That means blocks and parries with the entire arm, keeping the outside of the arm to the knife, using more than your hands to immobilize the weapon if you get the opportunity and choose to do so, 'shocking' the knifer with a hard attack after you have stopped the knife (this is not always an option but it can help you to re-position and re-orient more easily if you can do it) and maneuvering yourself or the knifer to where you are at least on the opposite side from the knife-hand or behind them and not in front of them where they will be best able to attack. The simpler the technique or tactic, the better it will be and the more likely you can execute it under the sudden-attack situation you will be facing here.

It's a hard reality and not comfortable to contemplate, but to ignore it is to risk setting yourself up for pain and injury and perhaps even death. Better, then, to contemplate it and what you can do before you have to actually do it against someone trying to kill you. Don't ignore the possibility. Give yourself a better chance to survive it by at least thinking about it before you might have to do it.

When you have time and space.

If the attacker(s) are outside of the thirty-foot line then you probably have time to draw and aim and engage them but it still may not be as simple a matter as doing just that. If they are coming at you they will be coming fast. The size and shape of your target will change from instant to instant. They may be crouching, they may be weaving around obstacles to get to you, they may be dodging back and forth as they close on you. There may be other people behind them or that come into proximity of them as they come at you. (Don't expect an attacker focused on you to notice someone else that is closer. They may well have tunnel vision just like you may have.) You don't want to wait too long to take the shot(s) but you want to make the shot(s) you take the best ones possible. So if you have time and can see a better shot coming, wait for that time. You may only get the one chance to stop the attack. Make it the best one you can.

The situation will become more complicated if the knifer is going after someone else or if they are running through or to a group of people slashing and stabbing at random. If that is what's happening and you chose to try and intervene (If you are with a loved one or someone that needs your help, staying close to them and/or taking them away are valid options that I will not criticize you for making.) then close the distance as much as you can before you make the shot. If they're struggling with someone or moving among a group of people the shot will be difficult enough outside of nearly contact range, much less any further out. So close in before you try. If you can get close enough to almost touch the attacker with the muzzle, do that. You want as sure a thing as you can get if you're going to be sure you can stop them from killing or maiming someone else. Don't hesitate. If you're going to try, go in and do it.

Whether you draw the gun before you start moving in or as you are moving in or at the point where you're as close as you can get will depend on specific circumstances that cannot be predicted. As a general principle I would suggest not drawing the gun until you're about to use it or unless you believe the knifer is going to make you their next target. If you are seen closing with a gun in hand, someone else might assume you are another attacker and take measures against you, or attempt to stop you from shooting out of some misguided sense or misunderstanding of legal and moral principles in play, or try to take the gun from you in panic. Also, if the knifer spies you coming with the gun, they could turn on you suddenly or attempt to use someone within reach as a distraction or a shield against you. For those reasons I would suggest keeping things out of sight not so much as long as possible, but as long as you feel safe doing it before you shoot.

There is also the question of whether to issue a challenge or warning to an attacker with a knife. If you are the target, I would not advise it. If they're attacking someone else, then it may or may not be useful to challenge or warn. A warning could get them to move away from their current target and give you a clearer shot. Or it could provoke them to try to evade you, close on you and attack, or use someone in reach in some way to prevent you from shooting. Circumstances cannot be predicted. I advise you to run mental exercises on occasion and 'plug in' some different variables to get a better idea of what your options might be in this kind of situation.

Other kinds of blades.

Knives are the most commonly-reported weapon in non-gun attacks by terrorists or deranged individuals, sometimes in addition to a vehicular assault. But machetes and small axes have also been used as well. These weapons have different characteristics than knives so some modifications of the tactics, techniques and principles of defending against a close-in attack with them should be considered.

With machetes the key points are that most of them are cheaply made (Don't assume the one you're facing is, however. Don't underestimate either the weapon or the person wielding it.) and that they are much better suited to hacking and slashing attacks than they are to stabbing. A solid strike with a heavy-bladed machete could do a lot of damage to a blocking arm. If you have to take the blade there instead of the body try to at least angle the arm so that it is hit at an angle instead of square-on.

When blocking or parrying the striking arm be aware that the mass and momentum of the machete blade may, probably will, cause the hand to bend at the wrist, which means you could still get hit with the tip or upper edge even if you successfully stop the swinging arm. (This is also true in respect to a hatchet/hand-axe strike.) This might change the angle/direction and position you assume when making a block against the longer blade as opposed to a knife. At the same time you want a consistent response that does not require you to identify the type of weapon being used before you take action. Choose if you can a standardized response-set that gives you the best chance of avoiding a critical hit regardless of the weapon in the attacker's hand. If you have to or are likely to take the edge on the arm (or leg, in the event of a low-line strike), do your best to angle and turn that limb in such a way that all you lose is skin.

It will be easier to get and stay 'inside' of the machete than it will be with a knife. The machete-wielder needs room to swing to get momentum on the blade. Interrupt that and you rob the machete and the axe of much if not all of their ability to do major damage to you.

If the machete-wielder knows what they are doing they will want to keep the blade in constant motion. They will not chop with it as if they are clearing brush or cutting cane in a hit-and-retract action. Even when they hit, they will pull the blade out in a different direction than the strike that hit, both to do additional damage and to get the blade back into motion as quickly as possible. This makes it harder to stop or trap the blade unless you know how to time, enter, and disrupt the pattern the machete-wielder creates with it. The knowledgeable attacker with any blade is going to be very dangerous and require extreme focus and, if you get an opening, full commitment to extreme violence in order to neutralize them or to get to a position where you can use the gun to neutralize them. The means you employ to do that can be simple but don't ever, ever expect it to be easy.

Axes (for now I am focusing on hatchets and axes used one-handed) will be more 'head-heavy' that machetes (some machete blade designs, however, will put more weight on the forward half of the edge) and so will have a more pronounced tendency to keep circling in at the wrist if the arm is stopped. You could try to put the block or deflection on the shaft of the axe instead of the arm holding it instead, but be aware of the possibility that the hard material could badly bruise or even break a bone where it contacts your blocking arm(s). (That is preferable to having the blade hit your head or body, however.) Like with machetes, a knowledgeable user of the axe will want to keep it in motion and will, on impact, rip it out in a different direction than the chop went in so as to create more trauma and get the blade moving again as soon as possible. The more you can interrupt and stop any movement of the axe, the more you will reduce the damage done even if the attacker hits with it.

One thing you must be aware of when you engage someone with a bladed weapon is what is called 'the myth of the one-armed attacker'. Many martial artists have been caught unawares by the focus on the weapon and doing things with the weapon-arm that comes as a by-product of the way empty-hand defense against a weapon-armed attacker is most often taught. The trap is to focus all your attention on the knife or axe or machete in the attacker's hand and move to deal with that, forgetting that humans are given <u>two</u> arms and hands. You then proceed to immobilize yourself in an attempt to hold and disable the weapon, leaving yourself open to the attacker's free hand. Suddenly, you are being grabbed or struck from another direction and are surprised to the point where the attacker gets the advantage back. And then, perhaps, you die.

This tendency to focus on the weapon is the one of the reasons (the other is the lack of facility that most defenders will have with immobilizations and disarms in the face of a killing attack) that I so strongly advise you to just block or deflect the weapon arm while dealing your own shock-damage to the attacker. It is also why I do not advise you to stay in front of them where they can reach you easily with either hand. Stop the immediate attack, shock and damage the attacker, get to the flank or rear and get distance, then take whatever other action seems appropriate to stop the attack or to escape it.

Be advised that this brief and the set-piece examples shown in the pictures cannot do more than touch lightly on the subject of non-weapon defense against a bladed weapon. I cannot express the need to get the right kind of real-fight-oriented training that will give you some capability against attacks with blades at close range enough. Even a single concept, well understood and well drilled, combined with full commitment could be the difference between you being able to get to your gun and decisively deal with the attacker and you being left bleeding on the ground while they move to their next victim.

The attack will be simple and brutal: The knife will be thrust quickly, in and out, like the needle of a sewing machine (the name and the technique of the quick series of thrusts comes from the prisons where it was developed). The blade may go back to the same place it hit the first time, or, like it does here, to another target. It will come hard and it will come fast. There is no elegance to this technique, but there is effectiveness. The kind of counters and disarms often taught in self-defense classes and martial arts schools will be difficult at best to apply against this kind of attack with any degree of success.

Your best chance of countering this kind of attack is to, if at all possible, STOP the thrust with a simple block or parry. Immediately or simultaneously follow that with a SHOCK attack to damage and disrupt the attacker. Then MOVE yourself and/or the attacker outside and get to their flank or rear. Done correctly and with full commitment, this sequence has the best chance of getting you to where you can access your weapon and engage or to make your escape.

Attacks with longer and heavier blade weapons such as machetes or axes will use more of a slashing, chopping or hacking action than stabbing. There will be no finesse here, either. The attacker will be aiming to sever limbs and cut deep into vital organs and arteries with the most powerful stroke they can generate.

Most of the power of the stroke will be focused along the last half or third of the blade's edge. The further inside that you can get, the less power you need to block or parry the stroke.

The principle of countering this kind of slashing or hacking attack is the same: STOP, SHOCK, and MOVE. Focus on getting position beside or, preferably, behind the attacker first, then on distance. This will give you the best chance to access your weapon and engage before they can adjust and renew their attack on you.

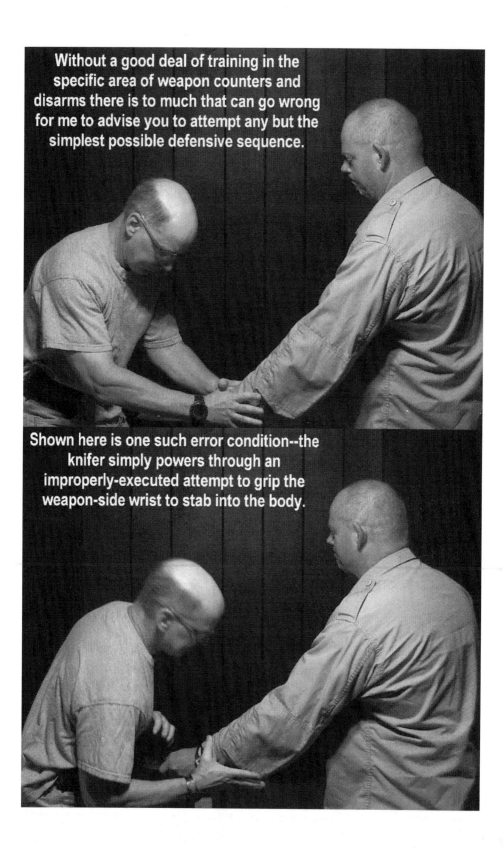

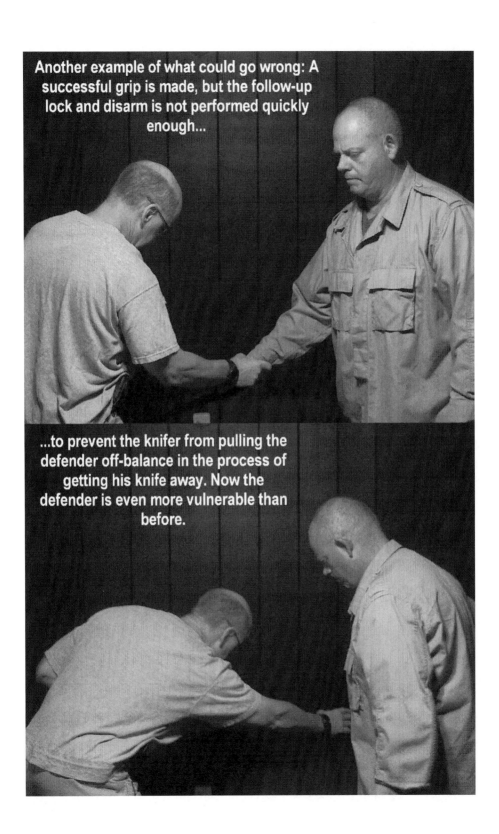

Two examples of the STOP, SHOCK, MOVE concept: In the first one shown here, the low stab is STOPped by use of the 'Dog Catcher' technique as taught by Marc Denny of Dog Brothers Martial Arts.

From the position of the STOP, defender uncoils and drives his forearm into the side of the attacker's neck. This SHOCKing strike is driven from the ground up using the entire body, not just the arm and shoulder alone. This brachial stun, if done with full power and directed intent, could render the attacker nearly or fully unconscious for a few moments.

Defender then uses the SHOCK to MOVE himself and/or the attacker to a position where he can get his weapon into line and ready to use. (Normally, much farther away than can be shown in this photo sequence.)

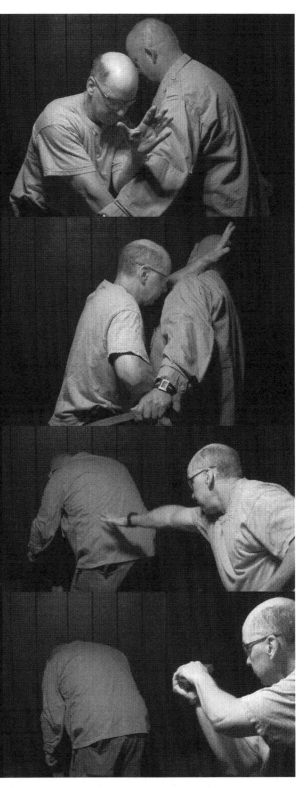

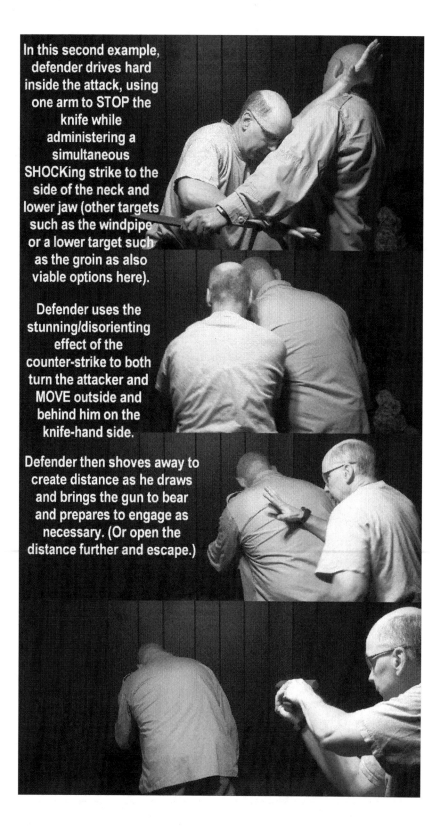

In this second example, defender drives hard inside the attack, using one arm to STOP the knife while administering a simultaneous SHOCKing strike to the side of the neck and lower jaw (other targets such as the windpipe or a lower target such as the groin as also viable options here).

Defender uses the stunning/disorienting effect of the counter-strike to both turn the attacker and MOVE outside and behind him on the knife-hand side.

Defender then shoves away to create distance as he draws and brings the gun to bear and prepares to engage as necessary. (Or open the distance further and escape.)

Any weapon control or disarm technique, especially one that relies solely on gripping and grappling, requires a combination of technique, timing, quickness, strength and, yes, some luck. Even many experts will find themselves at a disadvantage and in potentially deadly straits against a committed attacker that is not first distracted or weakened.

Simple techniques, applied with complete commitment and violent intent and that don't require you to grip, grab, or wrestle the attacker will help you stay out of positions like this and give you a better chance of stopping the attack.

Chopping weapons such as machetes and axes develop their killing power along about the last third of their length. If you can't get well outside of the swing, move in close to best effect your defense.

An axe or hatchet can be blocked at the handle, thought this will probably cause at least bruising. Blocking at the handle does prevent the axe from swinging around the pivot of the wrist and perhaps striking you even though you stopped the striking arm with your block.

Once the STOP is effected, ATTACK back hard. Do not limit yourself to just blocking the weapon. That just lets the attacker pull it back and try again.

When You Don't Have A Gun

Active-shooter attacks so far reported seldom occur in areas where even a low percentage of the general population are known or suspected to be carrying personal firearms. In some cases this is because of laws and regulations prohibiting such private carry in any capacity and in others it is because the business or organization that owns or has charge of the property does not allow it. For those and other reasons it is possible that you could be caught in an active-shooter event without having immediate access to a gun. For that reason it is useful to have at least a basic knowledge and understanding of how to use non-firearm weapons, including ad-hoc and improvised weapons, against someone attacking with a gun or with a blade.

We have to talk about commitment to the use of a knife or other stabbing or even a blunt object against another person first. It seems easy on the first look—"They're trying to kill me, of course I will commit to stabbing or slamming them with something to the point where they might die."

But are you sure of that?

Can you imagine driving a knife into someone's chest, ripping it back, and driving it in again as fast as you hammer a nail? Can you see the blood in your mind, more and more of it, as you repeatedly stab someone?

Can you imagine the feel of it as it gets on your hand and the sight of it covering your blade and the hand and maybe the arm that holds that blade? Can you imagine the feel of ramming your knife into the side of someone's throat and <u>ripping</u> it toward you with full intention to sever all the veins <u>and</u> the windpipe as you bring it out? Can you see the tip of the blade as it goes through the skin under the jaw on its way up through the base of the soft palate and into the base of the brain? Can you feel the point and edge moving through the resistance of skin and muscle and blood vessels, feel it scrape or bounce off a bone inside the body of the person you just stabbed? Can you see in your mind's eye the body of a man or a woman on the ground close to you spilling the blood of their body out because of the openings <u>you</u> made? Can you see the pen in your hand going into someone's eye and back behind it as you try to jam it all the way into their brain? Can you see the skin and bone of the skull caving in from the power you're putting into the tape dispenser you're slamming into them again and again. See the gash in their throat pouring out blood from the stab-and-rip you made with the scissors in your hand?

    Can you imagine standing alive and knowing that the blood on you is that of someone you've just had to kill?

    It's not the same as shooting someone with a gun and I'm not going to sugar-coat it for you. Sometimes when you shoot someone you almost can't tell that you've hit them. There's no blossom of red, no jerk or twitch, nor are they thrown bodily back like on TV or in the movies. Sometimes the only way you know they're hit is that they change their behavior or fall down or you see the blood coming out after they've been shot. The only thing you feel at the moment is the recoil of the weapon. Unless they're close you won't see their expression change (if it does) when they're hit.

    With a knife, pointed stick, stabbing with a pen, or hitting with a club or chair or other blunt instrument—you're right there, you can't miss it. You'll feel yourself doing damage, have to deal with them struggling to keep you from doing damage, see the results of your impact, feel the impact all the way up your arm and into your body, see their expression change as they're hit and hit again. You have to be <u>willing</u> to go through that and <u>able</u> to go through that if you're going to survive and win against someone with a gun or a blade that wants to kill you.

Go anywhere less than all the way in your commitment to countervailing violence and you might very well die, and everyone with you. It is just that simple.

Assuming you can commit to the messy kind of personal violence that attacking someone with a stabbing or cutting weapon entails, you want to make that commitment and that messy personal violence as effective and efficient as you can. If you've got close enough to an active shooter to ambush them with a knife you want to make the most of the opportunity. The goal is the same with knife or clubbing weapon or gun: Stop them from killing others. To do that, you need to do effective, fight-ending damage. To do <u>that</u>, you want to know where the best targets are.

With stabbing and slashing weapons the primary area of attack is the neck and head, secondary the arm(s) or hand(s) holding the gun. Take what is available if you can't get one of those and do as much damage as you can wherever you strike to but if you can go for the controller and its supporting structure. Given a choice, stabs are preferable to cuts—drive the knife or pen or stick in hard, go as deep as you can, and <u>rip</u>—don't draw it straight—out. Then do it again. Side and front of the throat to get the veins and the windpipe. Under the jaw at an upward angle to drive through the skin and mouth, into the soft palate, and to the base of the brain. Into the eyes through the eyeball and into the brain behind it. Stab as hard as you can, drive in as far as you can, rip out at an angle to open the hole you make up and tear and rip muscles and blood vessels to either side of the entry point, and either send your weapon back the same place or find another point and go in there.

If you cannot stab and have to cut, then follow the advice of Miyamoto Musashi and <u>cut</u>, not slash. Goal with a cut is to open the target to the bone. Move the edge as you cut—don't chop like it's an axe, cut and draw like you're carving meat at the table. Cut, cut deep, draw it back and do it again.

If you have to go for the arms, try to get inside the lower arms and/or across the back of the hand. Goal is to sever muscles and tendons in order to rob them of their ability to hold and move and fire the weapon they carry. But if you can't get to the inside of an arm don't wait until you can to cut. And take any opportunity to stab instead of cut. And always be looking to go from the arm to the head as soon as you can.

Cutting to the head and neck, side and front of the neck will be the preferred target areas. Aim to sever the windpipe and every vein in that side of the neck. Note that the blood vessels on the face and forehead are close to the skin. Slashing across the head above the eyes could cause bleeding that partially blinds the attacker.

You want to get close, in or almost in contact with the shooter. Use your free hand and arm to jam and immobilize their weapon and weapon arm. Manage your closing movement so that you don't slam into them in a way that makes them bounce away from you. If that happens, follow them. Get on their flank or behind them (if you're behind them, open the attack by stabbing a kidney, then go to the neck and head). You'll have to try and be aware of where the muzzle of the gun is as you hit them. Understand that they may trigger a shot or burst reflexively when you make contact. Don't let that distract you and don't be where it can hit you.

If you are stabbing with something like a pen or pencil be aware that it might break. With an improvised stabbing tool like that, go straight in and straight out and try to avoid any area where a bone is. Stab repeatedly as long as the pen or pencil holds out. (You don't need a special-made 'tactical' pen to hit someone with. Almost any pen, even a simple plastic Bic pen or equivalent, will allow you to stab at least once as long as you hit straight with it.)

While a larger blade may be preferable to a smaller one, you can still do more than enough damage to stop the attack with something no more than an inch in length if you choose your targets wisely. With short blades go for the throat and into the eyes first. From behind, you can still reach the kidneys with about two inches of blade length. You can also sever tendons in the hand and arms with a short blade.

With bludgeons or clubs, commit to putting every bit of strength and power you can generate into each and every blow. Think not about breaking but about shattering every bone you hit. Preferred targets will be the face and neck first. The skull is thick and rounded, but the bones of the face are thin and there are openings in the skull there that will allow for more penetration of even a blunt object. Besides the windpipe in front, there are nerves in the side of the neck that when hit can stun the attacker, allowing you to either immobilize them immediately or to set them up for follow-on blows that do. The occipital bones around the eyes and the cartilage in the nose—smashing those will at the least create disorientation and degrade the shooter's ability to fight back. And while the idea of driving the base of the nose up into the skull and into the brain is a martial arts' myth, smashing the nose will create pain and disorientation and distraction. So will a hard blow to the base of the jaw where it joins the skull. From behind, strike to the base of the skull into the neck where so many video villains have been felled by a fictional hero's karate-chop. Don't expect your blow to have the same effect though. The kidneys are also a viable target from the rear and will cause the attacker a lot of pain if they are hit hard.

Hit, retract, hit again. And again. And again. Until you are sure the shooter is not in condition to pull the trigger again, keep hitting them. You cannot afford to give them a chance to recover and turn their gun on you. It will be easier for an attacker to do this with a handgun than with a rifle or shotgun. This is one of the reasons that <u>you have to get close</u>. Even arm's reach may be too far. As much as you can when you attack, keep track of where the weapon is and be ready to block or jam any attempt to swing it around to point at you. If your own weapon is one-handed, consider using the free hand or arm to check and stall movement of the weapon arm and hand as long as you can focus on your attack. Try not to get in a wrestling match with them over the gun. Do damage, do damage, do damage. Get them thinking more about the pain and injury you are doing than about the gun in their hands as a prelude to getting them to where they are not thinking about anything.

If it turns out that all you have is your hands and feet and the body they are attached to, you can still win. Fingers can dig into and rip skin away and drive into the eye sockets and through the eyes. Fists can pummel and bruise and even break. The edge of the hand can shock the nerves in the side of the neck and crush the windpipe. The heel of the palm can drive someone's head back into a wall or other object as the fingers seek out the eyes. The side of the fist or edge of the hand can strike the Temporal-Mandibular joint at the base of the jaw to cause pain and distraction. Elbows can deeply penetrate the soft areas of the chest, into the kidneys from behind, or shatter the thin bones in the face. Feet can stomp into ankles and break knees. There are a number of ways a fully unarmed man or woman who is committed to decisively ending an attack can do exactly that.

Going up against a gun-armed killer without a gun of their own is something that no one wants to do if there are other options available. There is a reason why "fight" is the last option in the "run, hide, fight" mantra that most government organizations and many businesses require their employees to be familiar with. But while the gun does offer definite advantages, it does not provide automatic and complete superiority to the one that has it. Time and again, people without guns have overcome and defeated people with guns. What others have done, others, you included, can do. I cannot and will not tell you it's an easy thing to do. I will only say that it can be done and that you should never, ever, give up and let yourself or others die without a fight.

Commit to do violence when violence is offered against you, commit fully, and don't stop until you are forced to or win. Start, and do not stop until the other is defeated. It can be done. You can do it. Training will help and I cannot recommend strongly enough that you seek that training out. But without the will to act and to win, all the training and martial-class competency in the world will not help you. Have the will, get the training, prepare yourself and, if and when the moment comes that you must, act.

Can you do anything else when life itself is on the line?

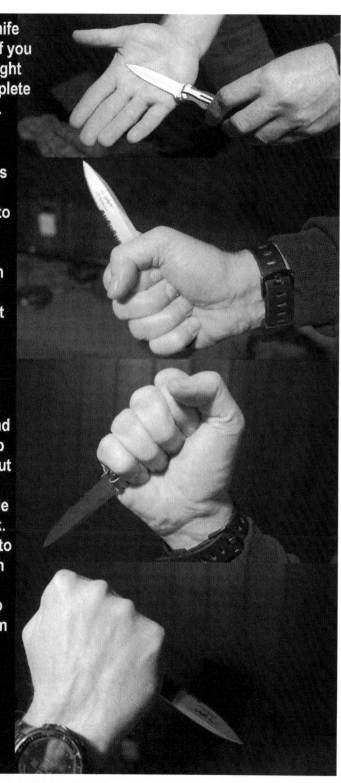

Even a small knife can be effective if you apply it to the right targets with complete commitment.

Forget fancy grips or fine control. You're not trying to touch them for points. Grip it firmly, grip it with the whole hand, stab hard and cut deep.

Don't try to get complicated or complex. Stab and cut, cut and stab until they stop. Put everything you have into a simple and direct attack. Commit yourself to a total effort with unwavering determination to fight until you win or die.

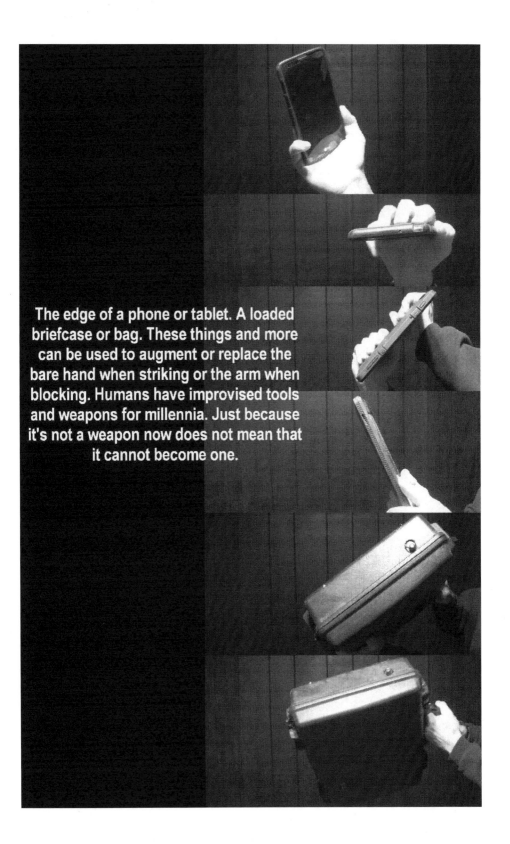

The edge of a phone or tablet. A loaded briefcase or bag. These things and more can be used to augment or replace the bare hand when striking or the arm when blocking. Humans have improvised tools and weapons for millennia. Just because it's not a weapon now does not mean that it cannot become one.

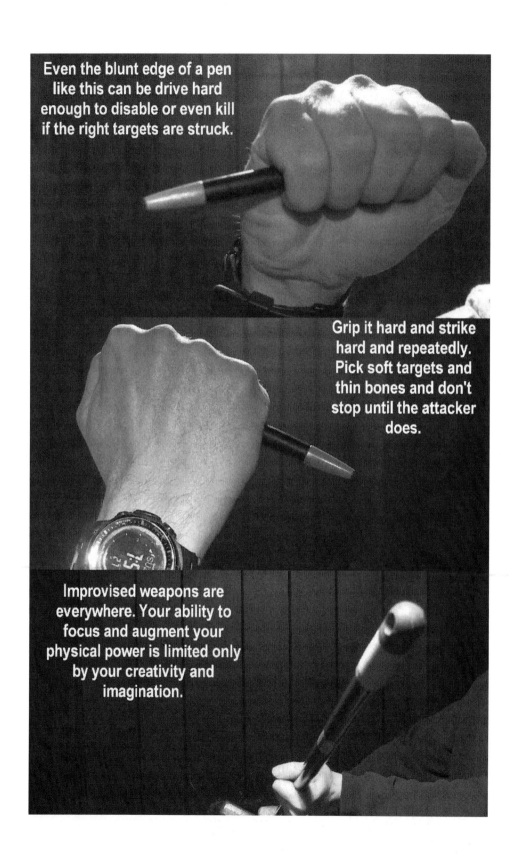

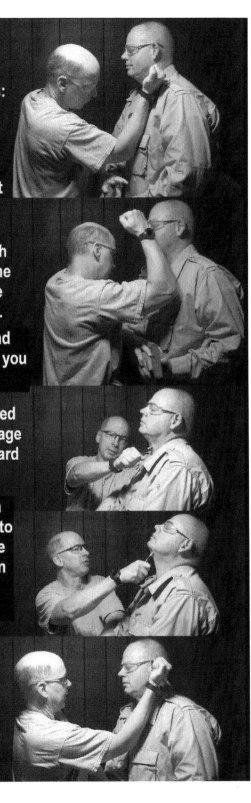

Examples of target points: Side of the neck.

Note how the free hand pushes the gun away from the defender and locks it out of firing position.

Eye socket - drive it in with the intention of jamming the knife or pen deep into the brain through the eyeball.

Keep their weapon clear and strike with as much power as you can generate.

Windpipe - even a blunt-tipped pen will go through the cartilage into the throat if it's driven hard enough.

Under and through the skin and jaw. Intention should be to drive all the way through the soft palate and into the brain from the underside.

Into the ear canal, again with intent to wedge the blade or pen or pencil (or whatever) into the brain from the side.

Intention and commitment is as, maybe more, important than weapon or technique.

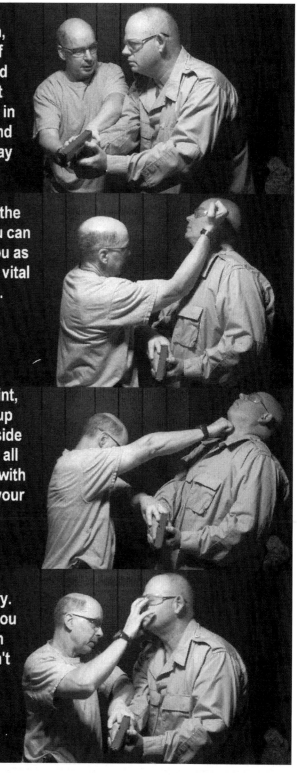

Priority against the gun, whether with a blade of your own, an improvised weapon, or nothing but your natural weapons as in this example, is to get and keep the gun muzzle away from you.

Get as much control of the gun and gun-hand as you can and keep it away from you as you make hard strikes to vital and vulnerable areas.

Temporomandibular joint, nose (directly on and up from below), the neck (side and front), the eyes are all good targets to go after with or without a weapon in your hand.

Absolute intention and commitment is necessary. Let up in the attack and you may die and others with you. Once you start, don't stop until you stop the attack.

General principles of striking include the use of soft against hard (edge of hand, side of fist, heel of palm against bone and cartilage) and hard against soft (knuckles, point of elbow, stiff fingers against fleshy targets such as the side of the neck or the eyes), using your weight and body mass to power strikes in addition to your muscles, and using small areas to strike with (edge of hand instead of side of fist, curled knuckles instead of balled fist, point of elbow) in order to focus power the smallest possible target points.

If you can weaken and distract the attacker enough to make a disarm possible, that's great. But don't be too quick to try that. As long as you're keeping the gun away from you, focus on damage, damage, damage until you're as sure as you can be that a disarm is possible.

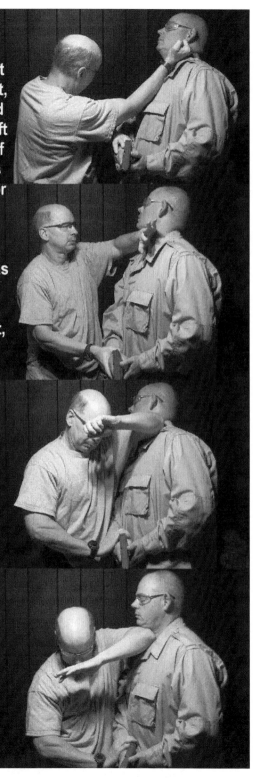

'Truck Guns'

'Truck guns', 'car guns', 'trunk guns': These are terms used to describe a firearm separate from your carry gun that is often or always kept in a vehicle. Usually this is a long gun, a rifle (pistol-caliber carbines fall into the rifle class as do semi-auto copies of sub-machineguns that can be found in the US) or shotgun. It could also be a larger pistol, perhaps in a different caliber, or a rifle-caliber pistol such as can be found in the United States. (For consistency I will use the term 'car gun' or 'truck gun' interchangeably for any weapon carried primarily in a vehicle that is intended to supplement or replace a carry pistol under certain circumstances.)

There are several reasons people can have for having a car gun. The one I will address here is that a car gun could be used against an active shooter. There is precedent for this reasoning—there are many examples of law enforcement and military responders using rifles against attacks like this in both the US and other countries. Whether or not those examples can be applied to someone like you or me, someone not a member of either of those communities, is the question.

I think as a general rule the answer is "No." Here is my reason:

We are not nearly as likely to be in close proximity to those car guns if we're caught up in an active shooting event as a police officer is who is responding to that event.

It's as simple as that. Unless the shooting starts in the parking lot as you're getting out of your vehicle (with the door still open), what you'll have on your body is what you will have to deal with the suddenly-developed threat. The time it takes you to at the least unlock your car, get to where you have stored the (let's assume for now) rifle, get the rifle out of the storage compartment or case it's in, ready it for action, set your position, aim and shoot, that shooter will be moving and shooting others or at you. Have you checked to see how long it takes you to get to the rifle and then make an accurate shot? How much longer is that compared to the time it takes you to draw the handgun you're carrying, get into a supported position, and fire an accurate shot? (This assumes you are able to shoot accurately with the pistol at the same range you use the rifle at for the test.) I'm betting that the difference in time is worth more than one life altered by the bullet of a committed killer.

It's easy enough to test this. Go to a range with another shooter where you can put your personal vehicle on or close to the firing line, set up two or more targets, and place a small area or point target on the one you will be shooting. (These targets don't have to be far away. This is simply a time-to-first-good-shot comparison, not a full-on accuracy test.) A 3x5-inch index card is a reasonable test target. Put your partner on the line clear of where you will be shooting from once you have set your weapon and yourself up to do so. You partner starts the test by starting at a steady pace to shoot at their targets(s) (not rapid fire and not slow and deliberate either, but somewhere in-between in tempo). When you hear the first shot, you must first look at your partner and count one second—this simulates your delay at hearing a shot somewhere and then looking to see what is going on and where it's going on at.

Then you will go and unlock/open your vehicle door, access your rifle, get it ready to fire, set up, and fire until you have hit your target with one good shot. If using the index card, any shot that is not on the edge counts. Edge hits do not count as accurate shots. Count the number of hits the partner made until that point. Repeat the test the same way but use your carry weapon now—it's up to you whether you fire unsupported or use a rested position (I would suggest trying it both ways).

I think if you do this test honestly that you will find that you can reduce the number of 'casualties' by at least fifty percent by responding with the carry weapon. (Assuming that you are capable of making the required shot. That will be a matter of training and practice and, to a lesser extent, how your pistol is set up.)

Think now about what is really likely to happen. You won't have only just shut and locked the door when the shooting starts. You'll be inside the building, the store or the office, and your car or truck will be parked tens of yards away. To respond with the rifle you have to get outside, get the gun out of your vehicle, get inside, find the shooter, and engage them (I am assuming you readied the rifle for action on the move. If you didn't, you'll have to add that step to all this.)

Now think what <u>else</u> is happening while you're doing this: The police have been called and they have been told that someone is there shooting people. They may or may not have a description of the shooter that is probably not complete or accurate enough for them to know when they see you that you aren't them. They will be on edge, they will be amped up, they will come in knowing they have to look for and deal with….

….someone that looks a lot like you do, moving back to or inside the building with a rifle in your hand.

That is the primary problem with the idea of getting the rifle out of the car and shooting the shooter with it. You greatly increase the chances that you will be shot as well. Don't get me wrong—you have the same problem and take some of the same risks having a handgun out as you do having the rifle in your hands. The risk with the handgun can be reduced and mitigated more than with the rifle, however. And you have a better chance of stopping the attack and then getting the handgun out of sight again before the police arrive than you do when you have to go out, get the rifle, and then come back. It's as simple as that.

Reduced reaction time that could mean fewer casualties from the attack and reduced risk that you will be mistakenly targeted by armed responders—these are important reasons to focus your training and preparation on using the handgun that you will have on your body instead of thinking and planning to rely on the long-gun you will have in your vehicle. There are other good reasons to have the extra gun in the car without making this one of the primary ones. Once you are as fully prepared to and capable of working with what you have, then and only then consider all the rest.

Examples

Here are some photo-examples of techniques falling under four skill-sets that I consider extremely useful if not absolutely necessary to anyone that finds themselves caught up in an activeshooter incident. Two of these, covert ready positions and protected/safe movement positions, are skills that I believe everyone who carries a concealed firearm should know about. The other two, close-in and supported shooting positions, are somewhat more specialized technique and skill groups where the general concealed-carry world is concerned though they can and have been applied outside of the active-shooter environment in the past and will be in the future.

Keep in mind that the photos and explanations you see and read here are intended to be taken as guidance and examples only—nothing more and nothing less. This is not a how-to guide and it is not intended to be one. You, the reader, are very-most-strongly advised to seek professional training and guidance to learn and integrate the full range of options that the photos illustrate only part of. There is far more to these areas of counter-offensive shooting than even a dedicated book could provide you. Training under an instructor who knows these techniques and skills and knows how to best pass them on to you, the student, is necessary to fully make these capabilities your own.

Covert Ready Positions

Knowledge of covert-ready positions is one of the things that all who carry concealed weapons regularly should have. The gun already in your hand, even if it is not yet on-target and lined up for the shot, is faster than the gun still in your holster. The ability to surreptitiously draw the gun and keep it out of sight gives you the option of being ready for something you think might develop but has not yet without making anyone in the area nervous or aware that you are armed. If the situation does not develop as it might have the weapon can then be returned to the holster with no one the wiser or agitated about your having a weapon. If a lethal-force threat does develop, however, you can be in action to preserve life more quickly. The parts of seconds you save this way could well make the difference between living and dying for yourself or others.

In an active-shooter situation the covert ready could be used in setting up an ambush for an oncoming shooter, during movement either to or away from a shooter, and in situations where you are not certain if the shooter or law enforcement will show up first. Covert ready positions allow you to observe and gather information without becoming known to the shooter, who would likely then make you their next target (assuming you are not the only target in their area of awareness) or having another good guy (official or not) mistake you for that or another shooter.

Covert-ready positions are as varied as your imagination and ability to use what is around you to help mask the gun in your hand. The photos here only scratch the surface of the possibilities.

Something to keep in mind when considering or deploying a weapon to a covert-ready position is the presence of cameras. Cameras, personal and private and public, mounted and mobile, are an all-but-ubiquitous part of life now. When you assume a covert-ready position don't forget about that.

Note: I am using pictures here taken from my recently-released fifth volume of my "Gunfighting, and Other Thoughts about Doing Violence" series, where I have a longer and more detailed view of Covert Ready positions including examples of how to present the weapon to a target from some of the common 'named' positions. For that more detailed view you refer to Volume Five of that series. And as always, I advise you to seek instruction about this and other aspects of fighting with a gun that you need to know.

This and the following examples of covert ready positions will show the position from each side and then provide an example of the movement of the gun to different firing positions in different directions.

Note how much of the gun is visible from each side in each case. This will help guide you about what position to assume in a given environment. Don't forget to consider cameras as well as other people in the area.

When bringing the gun to a firing position from covert ready it is important to follow the same rules about movement, muzzle direction, and leveling the gun as you do with the normal draw from the holster.

Keep it close to the body, don't level it until it's where you can point to target, don't let the muzzle go out of vertical until you're ready to level it at the target.

(For a more detailed discussion of the drawstroke refer to Volume One of this series.)

First is the basic down-behind-the-leg position. This can be either behind the leg as shown here or at the side. It hides the gun from one direction but not much more than that like most of the other positions you will see here.

Here I have the gun out of the holster but still under the shirt and am holding it with both hands. The last photo shows how the left hand pins the trigger finger to the slide in a variation of the Covered Sul position. To present the gun all you have to do is roll it forward and out, possibly with a short downward movement to help clear the shirt. If you have worked with Sul you will be familiar with that movement to target.

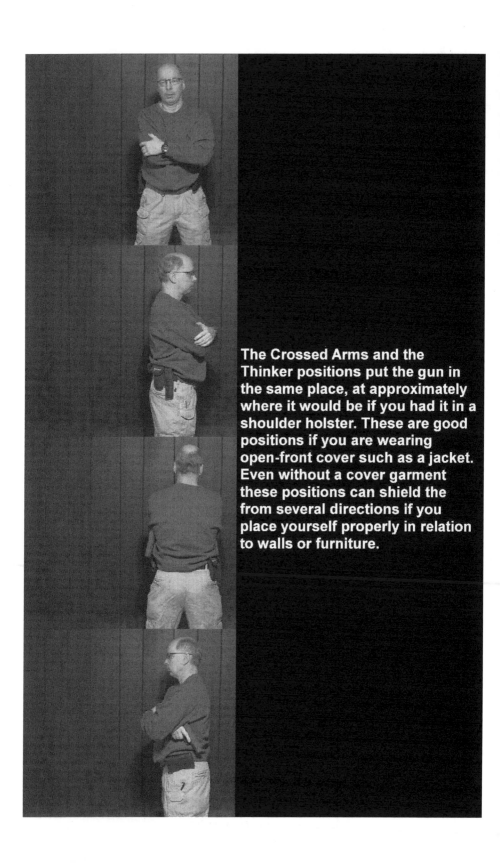

The Crossed Arms and the Thinker positions put the gun in the same place, at approximately where it would be if you had it in a shoulder holster. These are good positions if you are wearing open-front cover such as a jacket. Even without a cover garment these positions can shield the from several directions if you place yourself properly in relation to walls or furniture.

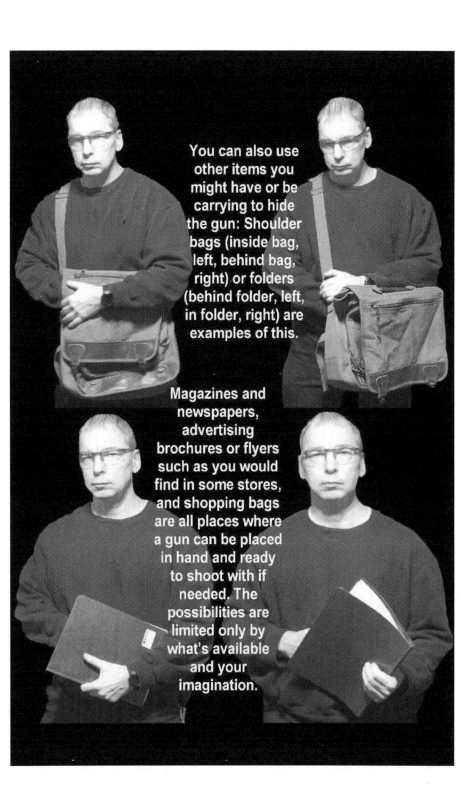

Moving With the Gun

There are two situations where you might have to or choose to move with the gun in hand: Moving through or within a group of people who are not targets and moving through an area where you expect or need to be ready for imminent contact with the shooter(s). In the first case you want to reduce the chance and amount of muzzle sweeping of people you don't want to shoot while you protect the gun against inadvertent or deliberate contact. In the second case you want to be able to shoot at the instant you recognize a threat that develops or reveals itself as you are moving.

This section provides some illustrations of the first case, movement through a group of non-threats. If you can, the best way to handle this is probably to get the gun back into its holster and under cover so that you can cover and protect yourself with both hands as you move. If the gun is already out and you have to displace against or through a group or you want the weapon more immediately available as you move but don't expect an imminent and/or immediate threat to develop soon (and for other times when safe(er) movement with gun in hand is needed), the Sul position shown here could be useful to you to learn and practice.

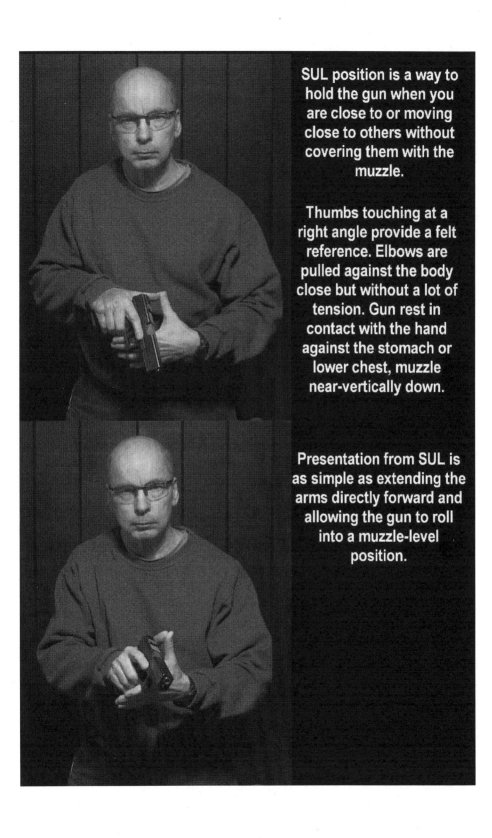

Support hand rotates into position and thumbs 'fall' into place alongside the slide as the gun comes up to the horizontal sight-line. Muzzle rolls up almost right on the vertical line of extension. Muzzle sweep is minimized.

With just a little practice the gun can be almost snapped into firing position and back into SUL very quickly.

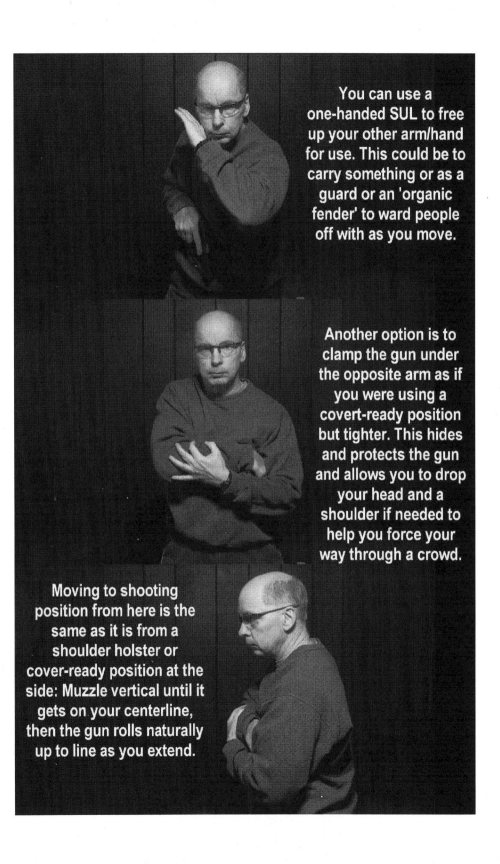

Close-In Shooting Positions

We are probably going to be inside a building of some kind if we're ever caught up in an active-shooter situation. Corners, hallways, doorways, rooms of different sizes, stairwells and other things inside a typical structure will at any given moment become both help and hindrance, advantage and disadvantage, assistance and obstacle to us especially if we choose to or are forced to move around and through them. It could be difficult to say the least even under more 'moderate' circumstances of escaping a fire or some sort of natural disaster that causes panic or affects the environment you're in at the time. Add in the threat of someone actively and deliberately trying to hunt you and others down and kill you all and you are defining a nightmare in progress.

Moving with the gun with expectation or possibility that you will need to shoot an attacker at any instant requires a different skill-set than does moving through a group of people that aren't hostile to you. The gun needs to be up and ready for use on the instant at the same time as you need to be able to see as much as possible and keep as much as possible out of sight as you approach doorways and corners on the way through the danger area. You want control of both the shot and the gun itself under circumstances that preclude standard arms-extended shooting positions or full focus on the front sight of the gun.

This is the realm of CQB, Close-Quarters Battle, and the place where the ability to use alternative sighting methods and positions that allow fullest possible range of vision, firm control of the weapon and reduced chance of someone grabbing the gun or directly interfering with the shot(s) come into their own.

Here are some examples of positions you could find useful in close-combat environments. Consider them as 'frozen moments' and not as specific static postures you assume. If you were to watch someone with training and experience with this moving through a building you would see constant adjustment of angle, height, orientation, and distance from the body and head as they moved. To gain that facility with this skill set for yourself, seek out qualified and knowledgeable instructors.

Additional skills you want to make your own in conjunction with this include the Third-Eye principle, the ability to aim and shoot accurately without reference to the sights on the gun, and the ability to use the gun itself as an impact and manipulative weapon. To gain the greatest possible chance of surviving not just this but other life-threatening attacks such as home invasions, seek out and take instruction. This skill-set is too useful and important to you to stint any more than you have to on training.

Note: Pictures in this section are taken from Volume Five of my "Gunfighting, and Other Thoughts about Doing Violence" book from the chapter on CQB. For a larger explanation of that skill-set and what it contains and demands of you, refer to that book. And this is one area of fighting where it is so very, very important to get personal instruction that I cannot overemphasize the need for it and the benefit from it enough.

Standard extended shooting positions are not the best thing for CQB movement for several reasons.

These examples are derived from shooting systems such as Center Axis Relock and Modern Technique among others.

Shown here are examples of close-in holds that will reduce your exposure and still allow you to keep the gun on target and ready to fire if needed.

These holds allow you to stay in a compact posture that reduces exposure as you clear while allowing you good visual coverage of the areas you are moving through.

You want to keep everything close to the body and the gun in the vertical eye-line at all times.

This should reduce your chances of being detected early, reduce adversary warning time as you cross a Line of Decision, and will hopefully give you an extra instant you can use to avoid a reflexive/reactive shot while you engage.

You can, if you want or need to, raise the gun to get on the sights.

Allowing the gun to tilt as shown here reduces tension in the wrists and forearms.

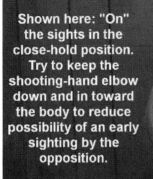

Shown here: "On" the sights in the close-hold position. Try to keep the shooting-hand elbow down and in toward the body to reduce possibility of an early sighting by the opposition.

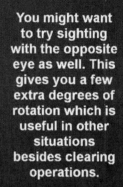

You might want to try sighting with the opposite eye as well. This gives you a few extra degrees of rotation which is useful in other situations besides clearing operations.

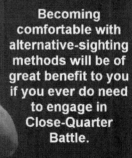

As you conduct your sweep it is advisable to keep the gun lower where it will not block your vision of the area you're clearing. You can still fire quite accurately if you need to by sighting along the edge or top of the slide.

Becoming comfortable with alternative-sighting methods will be of great benefit to you if you ever do need to engage in Close-Quarter Battle.

Supported Positions for Long-Range Pistol Shooting

However good you are at shooting a handgun at long range (defined for our purposes here as beyond 20 yards) or at making precise shots at shorter ranges you will be more assured of making a fight-stopping shot if you can somehow brace or support the gun, your hands and/or arms, or all three. If you do find yourself needing to shoot an attacker at a distance it will be better if you can to find something you can stabilize the gun with even if that is another part of your own body.

Look around now and see what around you could be used to support or brace your pistol with. Experiment with positions such as are shown here and others you may see as you expand your studies of counteroffensive shooting with a handgun. There are also a few trainers who incorporate modules of instruction in long-range shooting into their courses. Finding those trainers and taking that instruction will help you become not just a better long-range shooter but a better shooter all around.

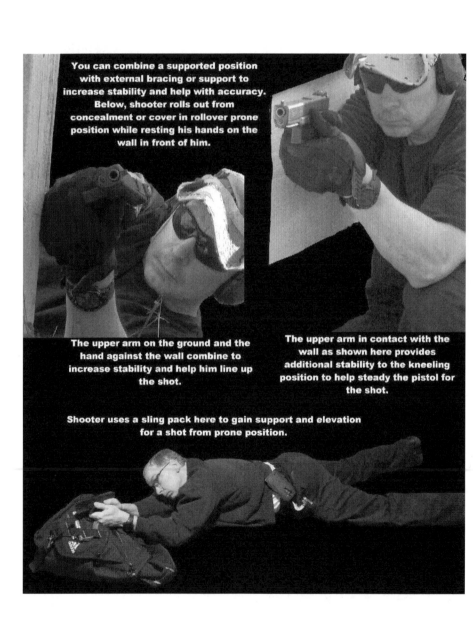

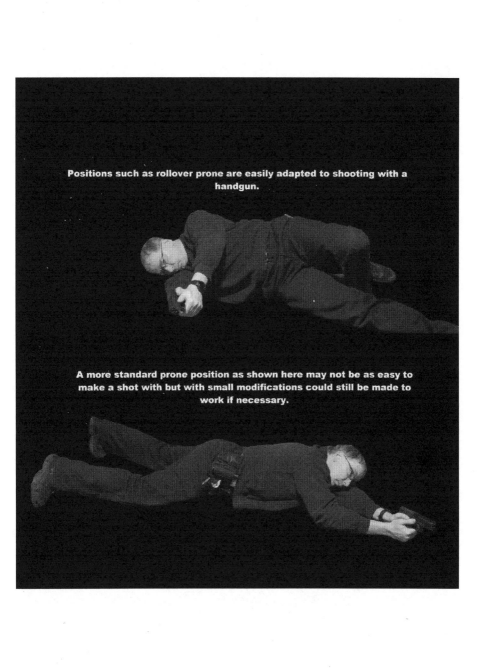

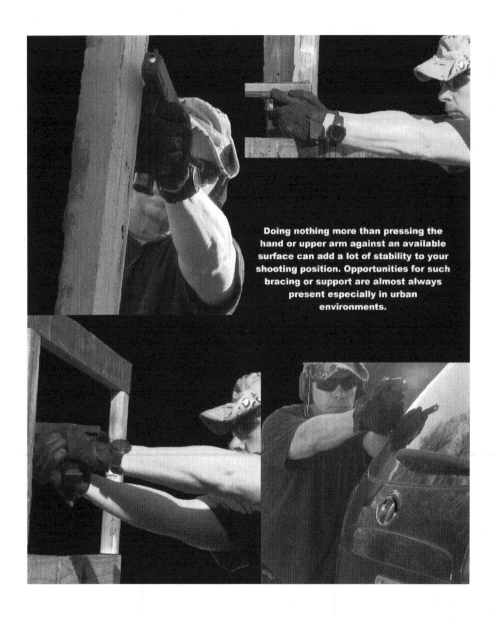

Doing nothing more than pressing the hand or upper arm against an available surface can add a lot of stability to your shooting position. Opportunities for such bracing or support are almost always present especially in urban environments.

FACING THE ACTIVE SHOOTER: An Outline of Tactical Options

The Goal:
Put a framework on chaos.

FUNDAMENTAL CONCEPTS:

- This is not a "normal" or "average" criminal act.
    - You cannot respond to it as if it is one. It is highly unlikely that a display of the weapon or a warning or trying to negotiate with the shooter(s) will do anything but get you shot. (Indeed, the cases I know of where a warning was given, that is just what happened.)
    - Only direct action will end the incident in your favor.
        - Direct action does not mean engagement in the context of this outline. This will be explained later.
- THIS IS NOT A RATIONAL ACT.
    - **THIS IS IMPORTANT:** An active shooting event, whoever does it for whatever reason they do it, is not a rational act. The event can be rational in its planning and execution. That doesn't mean it is a rational act. Do not let the appearance mislead you as to the true nature of the event.

- It cannot be thought of as a rational act even in the context of criminal action or warfare.
- The motivation of the shooter is irrelevant <u>to you</u>.
- Because it is not a rational act, it cannot be responded to with the same mindset or attitude as a criminal act or warfare.
  - You must base your response on the action, not the motivation behind it.
- If you think of it or try to respond to it as a rational act, you are wrong and you may die.

CHOICES OF ACTION:

- Escape
  - Get yourself and others out of harm's way. ▪ Includes going to a position of cover and/or concealment such that the shooter(s) cannot reach you or they don't know you're in reach.
- Engage
  - Fight the shooter(s).
  - Fight can become flight or vice-versa.
- "Fort up"
  - Find a covered position that limits access to the shooter(s).
  - Construct barricades and firing positions as time and circumstance allows.
  - Prepare to fight from that position if/when the shooter(s) find you.
  - Have/set up emergency exit routes if possible.
  - Gather resources as you are able.
  - Goal is to survive until responders secure the area and/or are able to get you out.
- Any of these options can be temporary or for the duration of the event. Any option can at any time be discarded and another option adopted.

- Recommendation is to, where possible, first seek cover or concealment so that you have time and space to evaluate the situation and decide on the best course of action.
    - This is a temporary stopping point/waypoint.
- Make a plan quickly and take action.
    - Do not wait for perfect understanding of the situation or a great plan before acting.
    - Waiting for perfection is likely to make you perfectly dead.
- Situation may preclude one or the other of these choices. (See PARAMETERS.)

GENERAL CONSIDERATIONS:

- Avoiding panic is absolutely vital.
- You will likely not know enough about the situation.
- You will likely have to act instantly or at least very, very quickly.
- You will likely have others around you who are panicking that must be tuned out.
- Communications with responders, if you can make contact, should be established.
    - Information will help them help you.
    - Expect them to want to direct and dominate the information exchange.
    - Cut off communications the instant it becomes a distraction or detrimental to your primary survival mission.
- Ability to adapt and flexibility in thinking are vital.
    - Proper use of resources available, proper use of terrain, lack of information and uncertainty about the situation demand adaptive and flexible thinking.
- Will to win, will to survive, will to overcome, can make the difference between living and dying.
    - Don't give up.

- - Don't give up.
  - Don't give up.
  - Don't give up.
- Important and useful capabilities and skill-sets.
  - Fundamental ability to shoot accurately and with consistent accuracy.
- Ability to shoot accurately while moving.
- Techniques of close-quarter combat, especially those specific to interior spaces.
- Ability to shoot accurately at longer than normal ranges with your carry weapon (normal as considered by most concealed-weapon carriers).
  - For purposes of this discussion, 20+ yards.
- Knowledge of how to operate weapons other than those you own.
- Knowledge of field-expedient trauma and wound care. (Immediate first aid of gunshot victims.)

PARAMETERS

Single shooter, in sight of shooter, close range.

<u>Engage</u>. Unless cover or escape is very close, you must fight or you will die.
- Ability to produce weapon from other than standing-in-open positions required.
- Ability to move evasively, draw as you move, and shoot accurately on the move could be the difference between life and death.
- Ability to place your shot(s), even on the move, will be important.
- If you lose contact with the shooter, you should probably not attempt to re-establish contact (go hunting).
  - Find a covered or concealed position where you can monitor the area, preferably with limited easily observable approach routes, and wait.
  - Keep in mind that they could ambush you if you attempt to find them.
- If the shooter goes down after your shot(s), make sure they are really down.
  - Observe them for a time. Be more suspicious than not.
  - Be prepared to re-engage at any time they appear to be going for a weapon or trying to reach or touch anything near or on them. The presence of explosive devices they are trying to activate cannot be discounted.
  - Displace at least a short distance and get behind hard cover if you can.
  - Scan the area around you after a short period of observation. Consider that there may be another shooter or someone who can remotely trigger an explosive in the area.
  - Don't assume that the one you see and shot is the only one there.

- Move to a position where you can at least see and if possible channel anyone else around you and/or to a protected position while you conduct an after-action visual sweep. While the probability of it being that single shooter is in your favor, you cannot take the absence of a second (or third, or fourth, or…) shooter for granted.
    o Check your immediate area, check your weapon to make sure it's still up and running, check yourself to make sure you have not been shot or otherwise injured.
- If you can immediately break contact, either through your own gunfire or simple evasion, escape becomes an option.

More than one shooter, in sight of shooters, close range.

<u>Engage</u>. Unless escape is immediately available, you must fight.

(Of course you may die if you do. It seems almost certain, however [because this is not a criminal act—if it is an armed robbery you will probably know it is] that you will die if you don't.)

- Goal is to escape the immediate area under cover of fire.
- The same skill-sets are needed and helpful as with the single shooter.
- Understanding how to flank and create isolation of individuals or smaller parts of the group by maneuver could be the difference between life and death.
- Absolute violence of action is required. You must apply the maximum possible force with the best accuracy you can under the circumstances.

  > "A good solution applied with vigor now is better than a perfect solution applied ten minutes later." – George S. Patton

  > "In war the only sure defense is offense…"—George S. Patton

- <u>Understand this</u>: You may die no matter what. No matter how hard you fight, no matter good you are, you may not survive this one. This is the most difficult situation of the eight that you will face. With many guns against your one, the only thing you may be able to do is, as Jack Rumbaugh of Suarez International says, "Give 'em the finger and die like a Viking." Your death, however, could serve to disrupt the attack and allow others to survive who would not have otherwise. Besides that, I don't believe in this case that you have anything to lose by trying. Given the odds of survival if you <u>don't</u> fight, I don't see you doing anything but increasing those odds if you <u>do</u>.
- If you do manage an immediate escape, keep moving for at least a short time.
  - Expect pursuit.

- If you find a place where you can set up an ambush position, you can pause there to evaluate the situation and form a hasty plan of next action.
- If you can, check and top off your weapon.

Single shooter, out of sight of shooter, close range.

Engage. You have the ability to end the killing right there and right now. Take it.
- Do not challenge.
- CNS (Central Nervous System) is best. A Center-Of-Mass shot may not stop them before they turn on you. Go for the Central Nervous System unless for some reason that is not possible.
    - CNS is not limited to the head. Severing the spine at any point will probably cause paralysis of the part of the body below the break.
        - The higher the better, but take what you can get.
        - Don't wait for a better shot. You may not get it.
- Distant third is to shoot the weapon or weapon hand/arm.
    - This should only be done if that is the only target you have.
- Ability to make the precision shot under stress and less-than-ideal conditions is required here.
- As you set up for the shot, as you move to the position you choose from which to take that shot, keep your eyes open and your awareness tuned to others who may be with the shooter. Consider proximity and behavior of those around/closest to the shooter you are aware of. There has been a case where the obvious shooter was accompanied by a (female) supporter, who subsequently shot and killed someone who was approaching the known shooter to engage him. It is hard to, but try and expand your vision as you approach and set up for the shot. Make sure the one you know of is the only one you have to worry about as best you can at the time and under the circumstances.
- Escape is an option.
    - Be prepared for your movement of escape to attract their attention

- Be prepared to engage at any moment until you are well clear.
- In most cases seek movement to the side or an angle off the shooter's line of approach or sight.
  - Don't move directly away unless there is no other way out and/or you have to move back a short distance before you can move away at an angle.

Multiple shooters, out of sight of shooters, close range.

- You probably have at best a few seconds to act before you are discovered.
    - You <u>must</u> make a decision and <u>act</u> on that decision <u>quickly</u>.
- Escape, engage, hold position and wait for rescue are the primary choices.
    - There will not be a single decision if the event lasts longer than a few minutes. This will become a decision loop that you will want or be forced to repeat as the situation requires.
- You will <u>never</u> have all the information you want or need.
    - Don't wait for more. You won't get it.
- You have to decide whether to remain where you are, move to another position or attempt to escape the larger area.
- Good defensive position? Cover and concealment? Ability to harden the position? A way to retreat away from it if you need to? Supplies and resources so you can hold up where you are for as long as it takes for rescue and recovery? A way out you can take <u>now</u>?
- To repeat: You won't have a lot of time to ponder this. <u>Decide</u> and <u>act</u>.
- If you choose to engage:
    - Set up an ambush.
    - While you have time and surprise on your side, set up first shot as CNS strike if possible. Engage others at best accurate speed COM after that.
    - Ability to shift targets rapidly is required.
    - Displace after shooting if at all possible. Move to other cover or concealment immediately after engagement and evaluate.

- - After engaging you must again decide to remain in the area of the attack or to try and escape or find a holding position where you can wait for responders.
    - Again: This decision loop will be continuous until the incident is over or until you are completely clear of the incident area.
- If you choose to escape:
  - Move immediately. The best chance of escaping will be in the first few seconds or minutes. The longer you wait, the lower your chances of escape get.
  - Be ready to engage as you escape.
  - If escape becomes impossible, engage. If you surrender, you will be secured and searched. They will find the gun and you will probably be killed. You may also be killed first if you appear able to give them any trouble after they have control of the area. (Adult males and older students were killed at Beslan and Nairobi for this reason.) You most likely have nothing to lose by engaging if they detect you as you move out, and you may be able to shoot your way out.
    - Goal here is to clear the area under cover of accurate fire.
    - Your gunfire may attract additional members of the attacking group.
  - Once you are clear of the immediate threat, move to cover or concealment and evaluate.
    - Move quickly away from your first stopping point. Assume that other shooters will be searching for you.
  - You may encounter incoming responders on your way out.
    - If you have weapons in hand, drop them immediately.
    - Follow all instructions given to the best of your ability.

- - Expect to be treated as a suspect until they are sure you are not.
  - Give them as much accurate information as you can. Do not speculate, do not hypothesize, do not theorize. Tell them what you know and what you are sure of and only that.
  - Unless they tell you to stay at or near the incident site, get out of their way and get out.
- If you decide to hold in place and wait for rescue:
  - Understand that you may be there for a long time.
  - You may be facing a similar situation as in Mumbai or Kenya-a large group split into smaller teams to initially strike multiple objectives or cover a large area prepared to fight for an extended period (days at least).
  - Besides cover and (long-term) concealment, you should also try and find or get what you will need to sustain you and anyone with you for upwards of several days.
  - Expect it to become a siege situation if the attackers are not quickly engaged by responding forces.
  - You must consider further encounters with both attackers and responding good guys.
    - Attackers may continue searching for people to seize or shoot.
    - Attackers may use fire and explosives against you in addition to shooting.
    - Responders will be searching for people with guns who they expect to shoot at them.
    - Responders may use flash-bangs, smoke, riot-control gas dispensers (grenades most likely, possibly sprayers or foggers of some type) and will conduct explosive breaches or demolition of obstacles and booby-traps as they proceed.

- It is possible that you will be caught in a cross-fire situation.
- Whatever option you choose, if possible contact police/security/emergency services as soon as it is safe to do so.
    - Identify yourself, describe yourself and your location, give them as much accurate information as you can about the situation. Do everything you can to make sure they know you are not a bad guy.
- If you are trapped or holding up, keep an eye on power if you're using a portable device (radio or mobile phone).
    - Make sure you are able to talk to someone at the point you think is the 'end game'.
- Arrange a signal that you can deploy that will (hopefully) be passed on to responders so they can know your location and not to shoot at you.

Single shooter, in sight of shooter, long(er) range.

- Immediate engagement may not be required.
- Option of escape over engagement is open.
- Immediate action: Move to cover or concealment.
    - Evaluate options once you are out of line of sight.
- If you are fired on or about to be, either displace rapidly or fire back or both.
- Escape option.
    - Unless shooter is moving rapidly to contact, take (a little) time to plan the route and movement.
    - Be prepared to engage at any time. (Shooter may move to contact deliberately or accidentally.)
    - Unless you a) know shooter's location and/or b) he is close, it is advisable to keep your weapon holstered or covered while you move.
    - Other people will be running too.
        - Think about and learn about how to move in panicky crowds.
        - Learn how to move with the weapon in crowded conditions.(Protected/covered/covert ready positions.)
    - Once out of the immediate area of the shooter, you can consider 'forting up' instead of moving all the way out of the area.
    - You may meet responding law enforcement on your way out.
        - Follow their instructions, answer their questions.
        - Unless directed otherwise, get out of their way and out of the area and let them go to work.
        - If you have a weapon in your hand, get rid of it immediately. Do not try to put it away. Drop it, get clear of it, keep your hands in sight.

- Engaging the shooter.
  - Choice is between move closer/to better position, setting an ambush or engaging immediately.
  - Move to contact increases risk to you but may end it faster.
    - Goal is to get as close as possible and to flank or rear of the shooter before engaging.
    - Try and maintain a fix on the shooter's position at all times.
    - Plan your movement.
    - Use cover and concealment.
  - You may have to move against the current of people running away from the shooter.
    - Until you are near contact or out of the current, you may want to keep gun in holster.
    - Know how to move with and protect the gun when it is in hand.
  - If shooter is seen to be fumbling with their weapon (Jammed weapons and fumbled manipulations have been reported in a number of incidents.) speed up and start the counterattack immediately!
- Ambush is safer for you but may allow the shooter more time to kill.
  - You must predict shooter's most likely route as accurately as possible.
  - Get as close as possible to the path the shooter is on.
    - Goal is a precise first shot and domination by fire.
  - Cover over concealment unless cover is much farther away.
  - Priority is getting the best possible first shot.
  - Set the shot up.
    - Supported shooting position if possible.

- Let shooter pass, engage from flank or rear if possible. Exception is if that doesn't give you the best first shot(s).
    - Central Nervous System over Center Of Mass on first shot if possible.
    - But take the shot that you are most certain of hitting.
    - You might can use the first shot(s) to freeze them in place long enough to get a better chance of the CNS hit.
        - That said, if you can make the surer stopping shot, do it.
- Fire until they are down. Maintain fix on shooter until you are sure they are not attempting to shoot again.
    - Be alert for attempt to trigger a bomb unless it is very clear that the shooter does not have one.
    - If you suspect a bomb and the shooter is still moving, continue to engage until they are not.
- Don't try for an absolutely perfect shot. Do take the very best shot you can.
- Be ready for shooter to respond if first shot(s) don't stop them.
    - If possible, have a fallback position.

- Engaging from where you are requires ability with precision and/or long-range shooting.
    - Long range is defined here as over 20 yards.
    - Supported shooting position preferred if you can get it.
    - Take as much time as possible to set up and take the shot.
    - Ability to apply fundamentals of accurate shooting under stress is necessary.
    - Be honest about your ability to make that shot.
    - If you aren't confident, find another position where you are.
- In all cases, be aware that there may be other shooters or others supporting the shooters in the area.
    - Odds are that they're alone, but the odds are not zero.

- - There is at least one case where a second shooter was present.
  - As best you can, observe others as you move to escape or set up the shot.
    - Actions of others will be your best indication of whether they are threats, potential threats, or bystanders.

Multiple shooters, in sight of shooters, long(er) range.

- Immediate action: Move out of line of sight and to cover or concealment if you can.
    - You may not immediately be under fire.
    - If under fire or about to be and not in quick range of cover or concealment, displace and return fire.
    - Goal is to break contact.
        - Don't make it a stand-up fight unless there is no other choice.
- Immediate goal is to get to a place of temporary safety where you can evaluate the situation and decide what to do.
    - You will not have much time to decide what to do and make a plan.
    - You will not have nearly as much information as you want or need.
    - You must act regardless. Your and others lives depends on it.
    - Shooters will almost certainly begin sweeping the area or building you are in. You will not remain safe or undetected for very long.
- Options: Escape, Engage, Fort Up.
- Escape seems most advisable in this situation. Get you and yours away.
    - <u>Act quickly</u>. This cannot be emphasized enough. The sooner you act, the more successful you will be.
    - First seconds/minutes of event will be critical. Group is consolidating control of area/situation. Situation is most fluid now. Don't wait until they achieve consolidation.
    - Make the best movement plan you can quickly and act on it.
    - Don't "wing it" unless there is no other choice.
    - Acknowledge that the plan will not be perfect. Don't try to make it so.

- You will not have as much information as you want or need.
- You will not have as much time to plan as you want or need.
- Look out for other parts of the attacking group as you move.
  - Assume that what you see is not all there is.
    - Better to be wrong than surprised and killed.
  - Find defensible waypoints along the path out.
    - Something you can fall back to if you encounter resistance or obstacles during your exit.
- Expect to encounter others who are also evacuating.
  - Understand the concept of "tactical triage". You may be forced to apply it.
  - Whether you want to or not, you probably can't save everybody.
  - It may come down to helping a few or dying trying to help everybody. This is an uncomfortable thought that must be considered.
- Attackers may have blocked or boobytrapped exits. Watch out of that.
  - If possible, have alternate routes and non-standard exits planned.
- Be prepared to encounter law enforcement response along the way and/or as you exit the area of the attack.
  - If possible, establish contact before making the final exit.
  - Follow instructions, answer questions.
  - They may take you under control and/or apply restraints. There's a good reason this may happen. Don't fight it.
  - Once you're allowed past them, get out of their way and let them go to work.

- Engaging:

- If possible, evade the group you see first. Go to cover or concealment. Cover is preferable but concealment may be better if it gets you out of line of sight and allows for further movement.
- Goal is to maneuver so that you engage the smallest possible part of the larger group at any given time.
    - One can defeat ten if the one can arrange it so they fight the ten one at a time.
        - Think guerilla. Think sniper.
        - Ideally, you want to set up a series of ambushes.
- Constrain their movement and their options. Expand yours.
    - Choke points, hard points, barriers. Use the terrain.
- Engage and displace. Shoot and move. Flank and infiltrate.
    - Where possible, have fall-back and alternate positions and routes.
- Avoid even odds as much as you can. Seek advantage before any engagement.
    - Gain advantage by position, by surprise, by movement, by...use your imagination.
    - Cheat to win. Cheat to live.
- "Battlefield pickup":
    - The longer the event lasts the more likely you will have to think about this.
    - Learn how to use weapons you don't own.
    - Using an attacker's weapon could put you at risk. Understand this.
    - Responding units may (you should assume they will to be safe) think you an attacker and shoot you.
    - What you do not or cannot acquire, where possible, disable.
- You may have an opportunity to convert the engagement into an escape. Be on the lookout for that option. (Whether you take it or not is up to you.)

- The longer the event goes on, especially if shooting is ongoing, the more likely that law enforcement will be encountered or seen.
    - They will be alert and 'amped up' and expecting trouble and looking for targets.
    - If you have warning, discard battlefield pickups, conceal personal weapon(s), move away from any known attackers, and wait for them to find you.
    - If you encounter them with weapons in hand, get rid of the weapons and surrender.
    - Obey instructions, answer questions.
    - Expect to be taken under control and placed in restraints.
- Forting Up:
    - Not recommended unless no other option.
    - Could be a hastily-cquired covered position or one found or constructed after breaking first contact.
    - Position has to be as strong as possible. A group will likely have rifles/larger caliber weapons and may have explosives and/or incendiaries and there will be more of them to shoot at you.
    - You may be there a long time. It may become a siege. As you have time and opportunity, set up for one.

Multiple shooters, out of sight of shooters, long(er) range.

- Escape is probably easier and the preferred option in most cases.
    - Don't wait until you see them to start moving.
    - Make your best estimate of their position and direction and direction of movement, but do it quickly.
    - Terrain immediately around you and your estimate of their position will determine whether you move to a temporary location and pause or move to escape immediately.
    - In most cases, moving at right angles or angling behind the attack is preferred to moving directly away.
        - Attackers may be moving forward faster than you can retreat.
        - They will be more focused on their front and those running directly away.
        - May avoid them herding you into a selected kill/capture zone.
        - Sets you up for a flank engagement with them more in-line than abreast if that becomes necessary.
    - If time allows, plot your route.
        - Set waypoints and rally points if you are with others.
        - Attempt to find a route that is not an obvious exit.
        - Set alternate routes if at all possible.
    - Be prepared to encounter other parts of the attacking group as you exit.
        - The group you know of is probably not be the whole group.
        - There may be separate groups of attackers moving in to the area from different directions. Be aware of this possibility.
            - As in Nairobi and some locations in Mumbai.
        - Group of attackers will often split into teams or pairs to better sweep the area after they make entry.

- - Reduces the odds against you in any one encounter.
    - This may provide an opportunity to you.
  - Know how to sweep and clear interior spaces.
    - This cannot be a slow, methodical search if you are escaping from an attacking group. Learn the difference between 'slow' and 'fast' CQB and how and when to apply each type.
  - Know how to move quietly or quickly as necessary.
  - Know how to fight in close quarters.
  - Be prepared to encounter others who are also escaping.
    - You are more likely to encounter other victims than attackers on the way out.
    - You must be able to differentiate friend from foe in an instant.
    - Understand "combat triage" and be prepared to practice it.
      - You may not be able to help everyone you come across that needs it.
      - You may not be able to help anyone but yourself.
  - Understand how to protect yourself and your weapon in a crowd.
    - Don't expect others to behave rationally.
  - As you go, note places that offer cover and concealment.
    - You may need to fall back or pause or "fort up".
  - Watch for booby-traps or blocks the attackers have set.
  - Consider other-than-normal routes for movement and exit.
    - Windows, weak points in the structure, roof or upper floor to ground. Things other than doors.
    - Exits may be either guarded or trapped or blocked by attackers.
  - You may encounter incoming law enforcement as you make your way out.

- Immediately discard weapons in hand. Do not wait for orders to do so.
- Expect to be put under control and into restraints.
- Obey orders and answer questions. Provide any information you can about the attack.
- In some cases, withhold information about your actions (but not about the actions of the attackers) until you can engage counsel.
  - Treat it like a self-defense shooting. Because that's what it is.
- If they release you, don't hang around. Get out and out of their way.
            - Just before you exit the building/area, discard or conceal any weapons.
              - Security forces may engage anyone they see with weapon in hand.
            - Attempt to make contact with responders before you exit. Let them know you're coming if you can.
- Engaging:
  - Do your best to avoid one-against-many. Maneuver to engage one-to-one whenever possible.
  - Isolate smaller parts of the whole.
  - Line them up.
  - A series of very short engagements over time.
  - Do not engage anyone head-on unless it's absolutely necessary or you can surprise them.
  - Maneuver to flank or rear.
  - Set ambushes.
  - Use of terrain is critical.
  - Always have fallback positions and alternate positions as best you can.
  - Hit and run.
  - You may have to use battlefield pickups.

- - - Understand the danger of this: Security forces could, probably will, mis-identify you as an attacker and shoot you if they see you with an attacker's weapon.
    - Know how to run common rifles and pistols.
    - Disable any weapons you do not take if circumstances allow.
    - Consider caching/hiding weapons and ammunition you cannot carry.
      - For later use.
      - To arm others with if you're on your own for an extended period.
  - If you can't go mobile, consider finding or making a hard-point and defending in place.
    - Based on known incidents, surrender will not offer survival.
  - Delay and disruption of the attack works in your favor.
  - If you have communications outside, tell responders where you are and what you are doing and what you know about the attack.
    - The more they know the faster they can act effectively.
  - Find or build hard cover.
  - If others are present, determine who can help and what additional resources to fight and survive with that others have.
  - Use what is around you. Use what others with you have (skills and resources and knowledge).
- When it's all over. (If you are still on-site/in area.):
  - Be careful of declaring an end to it too quickly.
  - Check for wounds and/or injuries and perform immediate aid as you are able if needed.
  - Don't rush out.
    - Responders coming in may think you are attacking them.

- Render weapons safe, get them out of sight and/or out of hand.
    - Unloaded, locked open (if they can be) safest.
    - Be as sure as you can that it's really over before you fully disarm yourself.
- Wait for responders to find you.
    - Understand they will likely be on edge coming in.
    - Don't make sudden moves.
    - If you are communicating with them, keep talking them in to your position.
    - Hands always in sight as they approach.
    - Expect to be placed under restraint initially.
    - At this stage, be judicious about answering questions without counsel present if you fired shots.
        - It is now a self-defense incident.
        - Treat it like one.

Vehicular attack, from directly ahead or behind.

- Initial response depends on distance incoming vehicle is from you at the moment you understand there is an attack.
    - If it's close (determining 'close' or 'far' in this case is depending on situation and circumstances that cannot be detailed here) <u>get out of the way first</u>.
        - Move directly to side or angle forward and to side.
            - Aim is to get inside turning radius of the oncoming vehicle.
        - If possible get behind or to the other side of something that can stop the vehicle.
        - Do not sacrifice yourself by staying in place to engage if it means you will almost certainly get hit.
            - Survive to fight even if it means giving up the most direct line of shot to the driver.
            - You may have time to move into direct line behind the vehicle after it passes to engage the driver.
        - If you can find cover that you know will stop the vehicle you can choose to stay at a shallow angle inside the turning radius to engage.
            - Staying close to the centerline reduces the problem posed by a shot on a moving target.
    - If it's far enough away you may have time to attempt to disable the driver.
        - Don't get so focused on shooting that you forget to give yourself time to move if you don't make the hits you need.

- If possible get a rested position. At least get the most stable and solid firing position you can before shooting.
    - You need more precision in this case in order to make a hole in and then get rounds through the front windshield.
- Do not try to calculate a different point of aim based on deflection caused by the front windshield laminate.
    - If you make any adjustment, go lower to where the windshield meets the hood.
        - This reduces the angle of impact of your shots and chance of deflection off the windshield.
        - Shallower impact angle is what you're going for.
        - Depending on how well you can see the driver, point-of-aim would be low on the neck or high on the upper body to achieve this.
- Fire as many shots as you can until you have to move or see an effect.
    - First shots will be used getting a hole in the front glass.
        - Still likely to penetrate, but will deflect more than follow-ups through the hole you create with them.
- The vehicle will probably not stop immediately even if you disable the driver.
    - Be aware that it will keep moving for a time.
    - Be ready for it to swerve/turn/change direction.
    - Get out of the way and get to cover once you've made an effect.

- Whether you cause it to stop or it stops on its own, be prepared for attackers to exit the vehicle and continue the attack on foot (assuming you are still close enough to the vehicle when it stops that you might become a target.)
- Be very, very cautious about closing on the vehicle after it stops.
  - There might be a bomb in it.
  - If the driver or passengers are still active, you might become their target if you get close.
  - Recommendation is to keep and consider getting more distance from the stopped vehicle.
    - Seek hard cover if you don't already have it where you are.
    - You must decide, if the attack continues on foot, whether you will or can engage those attackers from where you are.
  - For guidelines as to actions in response to attackers coming out of the vehicle, see the earlier sections of this outline.

Vehicular attack, other targets, crossing directly or at an angle.

- Decision to immediately engage or not depends on your understanding and confidence of your ability to hit a fast-crossing target.
    - If you can't make the shot, don't try.
        - Be honest with yourself about your ability to make a crossing shot like this before you commit to firing.
    - If you have time before it gets outside of your accurate engagement envelope, consider changing position to get a better shot on the driver.
- Side of vehicle will usually be less resistant to gunfire than front will.
    - Even the door is likely easier to penetrate than front windshield glass unless you hit one of the mechanisms inside or any crash-reinforcement material in it.
- You still should continue shooting, as long as you can make hits, until you can see an effect from your gunfire.
    - <u>To repeat: If you don't believe you can hit any more or know that you are no longer making hits, stop shooting.</u>
        - You don't want your rounds to go anywhere but into your target.
- At acute angles, bullets have been known to bounce off the bodies of vehicles and continue on at shallow angles.
    - If you don't have at least a forty-five degree angle to the vehicle, don't try the shot.
    - The closer to ninety degrees you can get before the shot, the better.
    - But the closer you get to ninety degrees the more difficult the crossing shot will be.
        - There will always be a trade-off of risk of misses against chances of hits. Your skill with the

- weapon can change the percentage of risk of the shot for or against you.
  - <u>Be honest about your ability to make this kind of shot</u>.
- If you have not had an effect and are still in range, option to move directly behind the vehicle and continue the engagement exists.
- No matter what direction you are firing from in relation to the vehicle, as much as possible you should remain mindful of others around the vehicle that are not in direct line of its movement.
  - Shots from the side, even with pistol rounds, are more likely to pass all the way through and out the other side if they don't hit the driver or a passenger.
- The vehicle will probably not stop immediately even if you disable the driver.
  - Be aware that it will keep moving for a time.
  - Be ready for it to swerve/turn/change direction.
  - Get out of the way and get to cover once you've made an effect.
- Whether you cause it to stop or it stops on its own, be prepared for attackers to exit the vehicle and continue the attack on foot (assuming you are still close enough to the vehicle when it stops that you might become a target.)
- Be very, very cautious about closing on the vehicle after it stops.
  - There might be a bomb in it.
  - If the driver or passengers are still active, you might become their target because you're close.
  - Recommendation is to keep and consider getting more distance from the stopped vehicle.
    - Seek hard cover if you don't already have it where you are.

- You must decide, if the attack continues on foot, whether you will or can engage those attackers from where you are.
    - For guidelines as to actions in response to attackers coming out of the vehicle, see the earlier sections of this outline.

Blade attack starting at or inside critical distance*

- *Critical distance for our purposes is thirty feet or less.
- IMPORTANT: THIS IS NOT A 'GUN PROBLEM'.
  - Inside thirty feet you may not have time or any chance to reach the gun before the attacker is able to stab or hack you.
    - Between fifteen and thirty feet you may be able to use <u>immediate</u> and <u>explosive</u> evasive movement to get off the line of the attack.
      - This might allow you time and space to access the gun without resort to empty-hand defense...
      - ...but don't depend on that happening.
        - Be able to defend yourself for at lease a few moments without the gun.
  - Focus first on keep the blade from hitting vital organs, then get to the flank or behind the attacker so that you can reach a position where you will have time to access your weapon.
    - Requires simple, stress-proof unarmed-combat skills.
    - Stop/deflect, shock, redirect, move.
      - <u>Stop</u> the blade from hitting a vital area, <u>shock</u> the attacker with your own committed strike(s) to vital areas, <u>redirect</u> the blade and/or attacker away, <u>move</u> yourself or the attacker to where you are in position to access your gun and engage or to escape.

- Don't try to disarm, don't try to wrestle or grapple for the weapon.
  - If you're going to attempt or get an opportunity to immobilize their weapon arm, use your whole arm, both arms, and body to create the immobilization.
  - If you get the weapon/weapon arm immobilized, immediately ATTACK ATTACK ATTACK the wielder.
- As much as possible avoid focusing on the weapon and the weapon hand/arm.
  - The attacker has another hand and arm and <u>will</u> use it against you.
  - A primary reason why you don't want to stay directly in front and inside the arms of the attacker.
- Get outside, get to the flank or behind, get distance.
- Goal is to convert this from an unarmed-combat problem into a gun problem.

o If attack begins at or inside of ten feet, you may be hit before you are aware of an attack.
- You may not feel the blade hit.
  - Victims often report feeling like they have been punched, not stabbed.
- If you are hit, START FIGHTING BACK.
- If you manage to stop the first strike, START FIGHTING BACK.
  - In this situation especially you must commit to direct and extreme violence.
  - Rip, tear, gouge, break, crush.

- Primary goal is to make the attacker distance themselves or create openings and distraction that allow you to change position to the point where you can access your weapon.
- Secondary goal (or primary goal if you cannot break contact the way you need to) is to destroy the attacker.
    - Unarmed at close range against a bladed weapon, lesser goals are a path to death or maiming.
    - Think 'destroy', not 'disable', 'kill' not 'stun' under these very dangerous conditions.

Blade attack, starting/detected beyond critical distance.

- Beyond about thirty feet of distance, you probably have time to draw your gun and engage them before they get close enough to strike you.
- Whether you do engage them or not is dependent on other factors.
  - If they are coming at you then there are probably no other people close by and you likely have a clear shot.
    - Whether and when you shoot depends on your level of skill and the confidence you have in your ability to make the shot.
    - If you do shoot, make sure that the attack has been stopped before you stop shooting.
    - Don't forget to move off the direct line of attack even if you do shoot.
  - If they are attacking others or if there are people directly or near to the line of you shot at the attacker, you may want to delay or refuse engagement.
    - Be very sure of your ability to make any shot you take before you take it.
    - If they are coming at you, displacement to clear the line of non-target individuals is the preferred option.
    - Waiting until the attacker is closer to better secure the shot is an option but not a preferred one.
      - The closer the distance before they are engaged, the greater the risk they can get through to you with a strike even if they are fatally hit.

- Move and keep moving off the line of the attack. Slow them down by making them constantly adjust to your new position.
    - If they are attacking others, you want to be as close to the attacker as possible before shooting.
        - Get as close as you can before you take the shot.
        - Be aware that the victim could interpose themselves inadvertently between you and the attacker at any moment.
        - Be ready for the attacker to turn on you if they see you coming at them.
        - Be ready for the attacker to attempt to use their victim as an obstacle or shield against you.
        - You may not want to have the gun in hand until you are very close to taking the shot.
            - You could be mistaken for an attacker by others.
            - The attacker might see the gun and react sooner than if you keep it out of sight longer.
        - You will be approaching a fight. Expect to see a tangled, bloody, chaotic mess. Be very sure of your target before you shoot.
        - IF THERE IS <u>ANY</u> DOUBT THAT YOU CAN MAKE THE SHOT WHEN YOUR TARGET IS TANGLED UP WITH A NON-TARGET, <u>DO NOT TRY IT</u>.
        - Do not go hands-on with the attacker in an attempt to pull them clear of their victim.
            - Risk of you becoming the victim is too great.

- You may have enough time to get away or get behind a barrier that will stop the attacker.
  - Remain alert and ready to engage if the attacker makes it past or around the barrier.
  - Concealment may give you the ability to escape or ambush, though a hard barrier is preferable to simple concealment.

After It's Over

The incident, that is.

You're survived the attack. If you did that by escaping and did not have to use your weapon, you will still likely go through a period where you will be answering questions from investigators and may be approached by members of the media. Family, friends and acquaintances will probably be anxious to know of everything that you went through. You may feel a desire, even a need, to publish something on a forum, or on Twitter or Facebook, yourself.

Don't do that right then. Wait on that part of it. That is my advice to you.

Answer the investigator's questions. Tell the media that you have nothing to say while the investigation is ongoing. Tell family, friends and acquaintances that you need some time to yourself to recover from the experience and process everything. Tell your Twitter followers and Facebook friends that you're not ready to talk about it yet.

If you talk to anyone immediately afterwards, talk to someone you trust without question to keep their own mouths shut about what you tell them. For a time, allow silence to be your shield against misinterpretation, misunderstanding, and misuse, deliberate and not, of anything you say about what happened. Fight the wish to get your fifteen moments of fame right then and right there. Given the nature of modern media, news and social and all in between, I don't see benefit to you from saying anything too soon.

If you feel any stress or ongoing discomfort as a result of the experience or if you just feel a need to, seek professional assistance.

And if you did have something to do with stopping the attack, if you did use your weapon at any point of it, <u>especially</u> if you had a direct hand in the ending of it, I beg you to listen to me and <u>say nothing to anyone but official investigators and even then have counsel present when you do</u>. You will do nothing but risk yourself, your reputation, perhaps your livelihood, if you talk too soon and/or to too many of the wrong people. Don't do what others have done to their detriment. Don't repeat the mistakes others have made. Don't pay the price they did for lack of self-control. Wait at least until after the official investigation is over. Wait some more after that. Speak only after pause, consideration, careful thought, and let some additional time pass before doing it even then. Pay strict attention to who wants to talk to you and under what circumstances they want to talk. Do your absolute best to manage and control <u>any</u> communication, however innocuous or innocent it may seem, however apparently trustworthy the one you're communicating with. Make it an unwavering condition that you be allowed to record any conversation and keep that copy of it. Talk under your terms and your conditions or don't talk at all.

Even then, expect your words to be twisted and filtered and sifted and re-arranged. Expect bits and bites to be taken from the whole. Expect the context to be lost. Expect it to come out at the end very much unlike what it was at the beginning. Expect that, and you will not be shocked when it happens. Expect that, and you will not be disappointed when it occurs. Expect that if you are going to give "them" your story. Expect the worst. Rejoice if your expectations are not met but don't expect anyone to surprise you that way.

Also, expect to be heralded as a hero and eviscerated as an evildoer at the same time if you had any direct role in stopping the attack. You <u>will</u> be both praised and cursed-of this I have no doubt. You <u>will</u> be looked at differently by some who you thought knew you. I believe this as well. And I believe this too: The curses will sound louder than the praises to you. You will hear the accusations and not the justifications. You will tend to focus more on the criticism than you do the admiration. Maybe I'm wrong about that. I hope I am. I don't expect that I am, though.

Know one thing, though, whatever else is said: Stop the killing and you have done a GOOD THING. Your action will have saved someone's life. Perhaps a lot of people's. Because of you, some will be alive that would not be otherwise. Know this. Be sure of this. Don't doubt that by acting you did the right thing.

Whatever anyone else says: You did the right thing.

Whether it was because you had to or because you decided to: You did the right thing.

Whether you were angry or afraid or both or neither when you took action: You did the right thing.

You did the right thing.

You did the right thing.

You DID.

THAT is what is important.

Resources

Train. Train the mind. Train the body. If you want to do the best you can in the moment when your best is required, train. These are resources that I am aware of that will help you.

Suarez International, Terrorist and Active Shooter Interdiction: http://www.suarezinternationalstore.com/terrorist-active-shooterinterdiction.aspx

Suarez International, CQB Fighting In Structures:
http://www.suarezinternationalstore.com/cqb-fightingstructures.aspx

Suarez International, Force-On-Force Gunfighting:
http://www.suarezinternationalstore.com/force-on-force.aspx

Dr. John Meade trains regular folks to perform basic combat casualty care and does a very, very fine job of doing it:
www.statdoc.com to contact.

Roger Phillips, Fight Focused Concepts:
http://fightfocusedconcepts.com/home

Dog Brothers Martial Arts Association:
https://dogbrothers.com/

Tony Blauer, the SPEAR system:
https://blauerspear.com/

Not as good as classes, but if you simply cannot get to one of those:

CQB Fighting In Structures DVD:
http://www.onesourcetactical.com/cqb-fightinginhousesdvd.aspx#.UmMEoxDUdhE

Mind Set: The Three Phases of the Gunfight DVD:
http://www.onesourcetactical.com/mindsetalectureonthethreephasesofthegunfightdvdbygabrielsuarez.aspx#.UmME1hDUdhE

Beating The Reaper!!! book:

Paul Howe, Make Ready With Paul Howe, Combat Mindset
http://panteao.com/product/combat-mindset-2/

Active Response Training:
http://www.activeresponsetraining.net/ A lot of good material here.

Like everything else in this text, this list is subject to revision as I become aware of other resources that will help you develop your capabilities.

What I Think Is Coming

That there will be more 'singlets', more single active shooter events, is a given. What I see coming besides that, sooner or later, is the kind of things happening in Europe right now:

A group of shooters hitting the same target from different directions.

Coordinated teams of shooters attacking multiple locations within the same geographic area.

Greater use of bombs either separately or in conjunction with use of guns.

Multi-layered attackers where a preliminary attack draws off or forcibly opens a hole in security which a second group then moves in to.

Second and even third bombs or teams of shooters set to target both responders and victims escaping from a previous attack.

More use of vehicles in attacks either as weapons, ad-hoc personnel carriers, or bomb carriers.

This is what I think is coming at some point to the continental US. I also think that these things can be avoided or survived if you are properly prepared and keep your head. It's not hopeless. It never is. It never will be. Remember that.

Last Word

At the time I write this it is less than twenty-four hours since a man opened fire on a large, close-packed crowd of people attending a music festival concert in Las Vegas, Nevada. He fired from the thirty-second floor of a hotel with either an automatic weapon, a semi-auto weapon modified to fire in full-auto, or a semi-auto weapon rigged with a mechanism that allowed the trigger to work rapidly enough for it to fire as if it were an actual automatic weapon. The attack occurred late at night.

Anyone in that crowd of concert-goers that was carrying a handgun would have required superhuman ability and skills to be able to locate and then fire back with more than lottery-winning-hope of hitting anywhere close to where the shooter was positioned. For all the rest of us, the only hope of survival in that situation would be to get to cover or away from the area of fire of the shooter. Nothing I have written here except for the idea of escaping covers this kind of situation.

That doesn't mean that everything here is now rendered invalid. Far from it. What it does mean is that there are no guarantees. Even in a situation covered here, even if you do everything suggested here, there is no guarantee, and I make no guarantee, that it will result or help you in surviving and/or winning against the attack. It is not possible to make such a guarantee. The reality of combat, of attack and counter-attack, of the chaos of that kind of fight, and of vagaries of chance, dictate that.

Do I think this will help? Do I think this will increase the probability that you win (however you define winning) and reduce the chance that you will lose? Yes, I do. If I did not, I would not have written it and I would not re-write it and update it and add to it the way I have and am doing now. Yes, I think it will help you. I do indeed.

That said, what I wrote before in this chapter still stands:

What History Says:

When an armed citizen has been present, there have still been casualties, but there have been fewer casualties when armed citizens have intervened than when victims had to wait for police to respond to an active shooter incident.

What Reality Indicates:

There needs to be someone armed, officially or not, on the scene if an active shooter is going to be either stopped early or prevented from acting in the first place.

What the Odds Say:

Official presence—police or armed and properly trained security (which is unlikely in the lowest-bidder environment that most business clients of security companies foster)—will not be present the moment someone starts randomly shooting people.

What You Can Do:

Study and train, not just for this, but in preparation for any violent assault against you and others. Prepare yourself for when you are armed and when you are not. Be armed as much and as often as you can wherever you are.

It is my hope that this text can and will contribute in some way to your study and preparation for this and other potential fights that you may find yourself in one day. It is my belief that it can or else I would not have put it together. I hope you understand that I hope that none of you reading this ever has to find out how useful the information here is to you.

Finally, let me express this wish for you and yours:

Live. Love. Learn. Grow. Prosper.

I wish you all well as you go about your lives.

CR Williams

Author's note:

As many times as I go over a manuscript there still seems to be some kind of miss-spelling or typo that I don't find. It's almost like they breed more when I'm not looking. If you find one, please let me know about it so I can correct it in the next release if not sooner. Thank you.

If you have questions or comments or want to discuss training you can contact me at crwilliams@inshadowinlight.com or through my website at www.inshadowinlight.com.

Other books by CR Williams:

Nonfiction:
Gunfighting, and Other Thoughts about Doing Violence, Volumes 1-5

Fiction:
Live Fire
The 'An Even Break' Series

My Author Page on Amazon

Made in the USA
Columbia, SC
15 June 2018